BIG JOE,
THE RAINMAKER
& NEPHEW LEECH

MIND YOUR BUSINESS!
THREE STEPS TO BECOME A GREAT CEO

RENZIE L. RICHARDSON

Big Joe, The Rainmaker & Nephew Leech

ISBNs   978-0-578-63593-4 (hardback)
         978-1-7348186-0-4 (paperback)

Published by:
BHFL GROUP, LLC
1954 Airport Road, Suite 126
Chamblee, GA

DEDICATION

To my children Erika, Daphne, and Quentin Richardson
(Half-pint, Dew, and Q-tip). You inspire me to live beyond my age.

ACKNOWLEDGMENT

I want to thank my family, friends, and clients who supported this project with their time and encouragement. I could not have done it without you.

CONTENTS

Make it your daily goal to live a quiet life,
to mind your own business, and to earn your
own living, so that you may lack for nothing.

1 Thessalonians 4:11

FOREWORD

Since 2008, BHFL Group (which gets its name from the initials of four great women in my life) has been helping companies solve their people and business problems. My name is Renzie Richardson, and I am a fixer, a strategist and a certified change management consultant, aka "Coach Re." I am a curious entrepreneur because I don't (and never will) do just one thing. My passions are helping entrepreneurs, business owners, and CEOs to be great leaders and have successful businesses.

I am one of the statistics read about in business news. According to American Express, in 2017, 58% of black women left Corporate America – I was one of them. Before I started my business, I worked for 22 years as a HR professional, and for the last ten years, I was an Organizational Development (OD) and Training Director. Ironically, I was bullied and forced out by a VP and the Chief Human Resources Officer – both men. What's more ironic, the Chief Officer was a client – he contracted me to investigate a senior director who was bullying his staff. I mitigated a very complex problem and was offered the OD and training director position, and left Atlanta to relocate to Birmingham, Alabama. I was brought in to develop a leadership training program. The program received rave reviews by the trainees and key stakeholders

— a dynamic group of regional vice presidents. In short, because of bullying, I was carted out of my office to the ER for stress and high blood pressure — despite my healthy diet and daily exercise.

But God sent me an angel, and he was a doctor from Africa. He told me a story about courage while he checked my vital signs. After he finished, he said, "My friend, you don't need pills...you just need to find the courage to spread your wings and fly...fly high!" The following day, I packed my car and returned to Atlanta to relaunch my business with a few thousand dollars — enough for a down payment on a place to stay. My story is an adventure and triumphant, but that's not what this book is about. This book is for you.

You will notice a few Bible verses I heard many Sundays in church and still live by today. I believe they were written for entrepreneurs. Be forewarned that there is one four-letter word that describes the mess we create when we lose our way.

For the last ten years, I have trained and coached entrepreneurs and executive leaders. My clients are black, white, Latinos, and women who are federal contractors and business owners. The things I've seen and lessons learned about running a business have been eye-popping. The causes of failed leadership I've witnessed are not in a textbook, or case study, and not shared in panel discussions — this shit is hidden. Maybe they are conversations among close friends or laid at the altar of prayer, but these fatal mistakes are invisible. How often do you hear news about how mismanagement, disloyalty, and infighting led to the demise of a company, or candid interviews about fatal mistakes to avoid? How do we help the next generation of black entrepreneurs? We need to know the back story — untold stories — to help the next generation to learn from past mistakes. We need to know, "S/he had a multi-million-dollar company, lost it all, and now not a pot to piss in." What happened?!

Finding the truth about how black entrepreneurs failed is hidden behind masks, swag, bravado, and naïveté. As I researched and spoke to black entrepreneurs, I was surprised that there are few stories or case studies about black businesses' failure, redemption, and triumph. There are a lot of publications, by blacks and other voices, about black startups, success stories, and downfalls due to lack of funding or socioeconomics. But it's hard to find stories that speak the raw truth about the shit black business owners do that puts them out of business. We don't have conversations about critical mistakes that killed the dream – we don't share lessons learned. What lessons can we learn from the Johnson Publishing Company – one of the most successful black-owned corporations in U.S. history – filing for Chapter 7 bankruptcy? What lessons can we learn from Essence Magazine, which was sold to Time, Inc? For the modern black entrepreneur, I want to facilitate a shift in sharing lessons learned – the good, the bad, and the ugly.

WHAT'S THIS BOOK ABOUT?

Is your business in the toilet, and you can't find your way out? The revenue is almost in the red, profits have flatlined, customers are leaving, and you laid off employees or contractors because you can't cover the expense.

I've been there, and so have many others. You are not alone.

This book is for anybody in business, who wants to start a business, or just outright faking it knowing their company is in the toilet. One thing I know for sure is that until you own your mistakes, your business will not fix itself on its own. It takes more than faith.

How many Sundays have we heard this scripture – *"For as the body without the spirit is dead, so faith without works is dead also. – James 2:26."*

We have to do the work.

I am a baby boomer. Back in the day, *faith* brought us through the Civil Rights Era and kept us hopeful for a better tomorrow – but we did the work. We held on to our faith because it was the one thing that led us towards the things we hope for – freedom, equality, prosperity, and abundance. What drives you to push through trials, tribulations, and losses? Faith is not enough – we have to change old, outdated mindsets and do the work.

SUGAR COATING NEVER WORKS

What I share in this book are lessons I've learned as a consultant, fixer, and coach. My clients are business owners who are rolling in millions, those who lost millions, and those who are trying to make their first million. What I know is that there are themes or patterns that are the substance of who we are – they either serve or impede our greatness. If the patterns or themes hinder your personal growth, they will also inhibit the growth of your business. If they serve your greatness, how do you expand your curiosity to continue to evolve?

Most of today's bestselling business authors write about good examples, success, positive-thinking, inspiration, and aspirations. These books are fine, and they leave you feeling good, but if you have serious problems, you are still left feeling frustrated. It's nice to feel good, but it doesn't tell you how to fix the fatal mistakes, and when the feel-good fades away, the same pile of shit is still there. I believe learning from others' fatal errors, coupled with solutions, leave a lasting impression. In my approach, the gloves come off.

This book is raw and will arouse those pain points that keep you up at night.

WHY YOU NEED THIS BOOK

Whether you are rolling in millions, have lost millions, or trying to make your first million, and you made it past the five-year milestone – this book is for you. I know you can avoid the fatal mistakes, but you have to be willing to change your way of thinking and do the work! This book offers thought-provoking activities to help you turn around your business.

This book isn't only for the business owner whose business is in the toilet or have squandered their fortune, but for the business owner who aspires to have a profitable one. The roadmap and exercises offer strategies to implement and manage your success – how to pick yourself up, fix the problems, and change to rise to new heights.

Wherever you are on the spectrum, this book has lessons wrapped in storytelling. Instead of writing this book in an academic approach, I think you will find it more engaging as a story – who doesn't like a great story? The characters are:

- Big Joe – the CEO and main character – the protagonist
- *The Rainmaker* – The CFO – Big Joe's Golden Goose

- Nephew Leech – Big Joe's "yes-man" – this cat is selfish and takes more than he gives

I hope this story will inspire you to read the entire book, do the activities, and encourage you to be a more mindful, heart-centered leader! And, if you are knee-deep in shit, I hope the lessons will give you a blueprint to repair your company.

Finally, I hope this book will help women and anyone who wants to own a million-dollar business – it truly is possible.

IT'S IN OUR BONES

As a child growing up in the '60s, during the Civil Rights era, black folk in my neighborhood struggled to earn a living and often did servant jobs like cleaning, housekeeping, dishwashing, and trash collecting – barely able to etch out a living of sustenance. I didn't know about African-Americans who survived slavery and became successful business owners. In my neighborhood, we had four business owners – a doctor, a dentist, a drug store owner, and Sonny, the Shoe-shine Man.

Our rich legacy is borne from the ashes of slaves and sharecroppers who became entrepreneurs, like Alonzo Herndon, Madame CJ Walker, and politicians like Maynard Jackson, who opened doors for African-Americans to access great contract opportunities negotiated by his administration.

Resilience, practicality, creativity, hardworkingness, and innovation, along with prayer and faith, were the backbones of the early black farmers and pioneers who became business owners. They developed their strengths under constant threat, lack, and stress – they made a way out of nothing. Harsh conditions forced them to work tirelessly to make a better life and leave a legacy for future generations. They built heritage and wealth from the fruit of their labor and intellect – no one succeeded without the help of others.

This book is written to remind us of our goodness, triumph, resilience, talent, and the spirit of community that forged black business people to build wealth and economic independence. We come from a heritage that birthed Tulsa's Black Wall Street, Atlanta Life Insurance Company, and Atlanta's "Sweet Auburn" – the "richest Negro street in the World." We stand on the shoulders of a rich legacy.

THE FALL DOWN

According to a study conducted by Guidant Financial of small businesses, there are 2.6 million African-American–owned businesses in the U.S. Since December 2018, African-American small business owners have increased by a staggering 400% in just a year.

According to the 2017 Bureau of Labor Statistics data, in general, about 20% of black-owned small businesses fail in their first year, and 50% fail in their fifth year.

Today, by breaking down barriers through education, access to capital, and minority set-aside programs in the federal and private markets, black businesses have a better start. But equally, black businesses are three times likely to close their doors in two years or less, and mature black companies are likely to file bankruptcy or sell out.

My clients are diverse. In most cases, I get a call when the business is almost on life support, or from the proactive business owner who is desperate to know the health of his or her business, people, and finances. A list of fatal mistakes and behaviors I have discovered are:

- The business is a hobby
- The company exists to support a lifestyle

- Lack of capital
- Greed
- Lack of Integrity
- Micro-management
- Mismanagement of revenue
- The business is a charity
- Stuck in the Status Quo
- Fear of change
- Poor leadership
- Relegating power and authority
- Lack of respect for human capital
- Disengagement
- Poor money management
- Denial and faithfulness to a fault

Except for two, all these mistakes can be fixed to put your company on an upward path to profits. If your business is a hobby or a charity, save yourself some time – quit.

Taking on a client for any one of these reasons – and they all impact the bottom line – is intensive, physically, and emotionally, for both the client and myself. But I love what I do. It is rewarding to take a company from ruins to profits. It is exhilarating to see a client do the work, and step out of their shit into new and rewarding ways of leading, building, and working for profits. As a coach and trainer, every milestone my clients achieved is a step towards transformation for success.

To share BHFL's approach, I'll use a project – Big Joe – a real client whose name I changed to protect his identity. Big Joe is a black business owner, the CEO of *Anywhere Logistics Solutions (fictitious name),* and has been in business for more than 15 years providing transportation and logistics services to city and county governments; and, federal agencies earning more than $40 million a year. For all the lean years of scraping and begging to keep his company afloat, Big Joe finally landed his first big contract – $10 million dollars. His win was a classic rag to riches story. He celebrated having money in the bank and, finally, a windfall. He loved being able to afford the comforts of life – he believed he earned and deserved the privileges of success. Big Joe became known in his circle of elite friends as a "*high roller.*"

But good fortune is not infinite.

While Joe was on one of his extended trips, his second in command decided to seize an opportunity that should have been Big Joe's re-bid for the $30 million contract – he was the incumbent. While Big Joe was globetrotting, his trusted right-hand man – "*the Rainmaker*" – set up a new company in his name. When the solicitation was released for a recompete, the Rainmaker responded under his company's name. He took advantage of Big Joe's intellectual property, pricing, and information he learned as the contract administrator. The Rainmaker wrote the bid and knew the profit margins to offer a more competitive bid.

Big Joe loved to brag about his "*Rainmake*r." He also called him his *golden goose* – he was humble, a well-respected CFO known by contracting officers. He had a solid network of funders and could walk into any bank and get a line of credit. Big Joe left everything up to the Rainmaker to run the company. He never questioned any decisions he made to bring money to the bottom line, but forbade him from approving any raises or bonuses, regardless of how profitable the company was performing. Big Joe always reminded the Rainmaker, "I'm the only Dawg up in here who can get a raise." The Rainmaker disagreed but seldom pushed back on Joe because he didn't want to the wrath of his anger – it kept everyone in check. Those who challenged him were fired on the spot, humiliating the person publicly to let everyone know what would happen to them if they decided to test him. One of Big Joe's sayings is, "to be loved is to be feared."

This time, while Big Joe was on an extended trip, his absence was a fatal mistake. When Big Joe found out that his company did not re-bid the contract, it was too late to contact the contracting officer or the program director – the contract was awarded to not one of his competitors, but a new company he'd never heard of in his circles. When he called the contracting officers, they wouldn't take his calls. As devastating the news, it did not lure him into cutting his travels short. Instead, Big Joe planned to teach the Rainmaker a lesson by taking a month's pay. The loss of the contract was a bad hit, but he would squeeze the Rainmaker to work his relationships to win a bigger deal to cover the damage – *the Rainmaker was his golden goose.*

Finally, Big Joe found out who won the contract award. He was on a yacht he chartered in the South of France to explore the Mediterranean Sea and Italy. When he finally returned stateside, his email inbox was jammed full of messages from his nephew, *Leech.* All the emails were the same: "Big Joe…Man, where were you?" "Why don't you take my calls or returned my emails?" "Dude, you are done, your shit is done!" In a panic, Big Joe called Leech. Frantically, he explained the crisis and what happened while he was away.

Seething with anger, Big Joe found out his second in command – *The Rainmaker* – set up a new company and took 70% of his employees with him. The few employees left behind were most of Big Joe's relatives, his loyal executive assistant, and a few loyal employees who he called dead weight – they were weighing the company down and added little value. Big Joe was shocked by what he heard. Big Joe couldn't believe *the Rainmaker* – his golden goose – had the guts to stab him in the back like this.

Big Joe flew back to Atlanta on Sunday and went to the office early Monday morning. He found the company in shambles – some offices were vacated, files drawers disheveled, and keys left on the desks of the

Rainmaker and the people who went with him. He contacted his attorney and attempted to sue his *Rainmaker,* but he was advised it would be a waste of time. Big Joe had made a fatal mistake by failing to put agreements and security in place to protect his interests. He attempted to talk to the employees who followed the Rainmaker, but they all were loyal to the golden goose. When Big Joe asked about what they knew and why they left, their answer was like a chorus: "I don't know nothing, and I found a great job with a great company" was the tune they all sang. With no contract opportunities in the pipeline, Big Joe realized the loss of a $30 million contract would cripple the business.

> Everything negative – pressure, challenges –
> is all an opportunity for me to rise.
>
> **Kobe Bryant**

BIG JOE, CEO

Monday afternoon, I got a call from Big Joe. He was referred by another customer, George. Sounding pressed for time, Big Joe stated his company was in crisis, and he needed help to save it. I told him I would drop by to discuss.

As Big Joe sat across from me looking stricken with pain and despair, I understood that look, but I could not feel sorry – it wouldn't serve him. If he had minded his business and key relationships with the contracting officer and program manager, perhaps they would have said something when he didn't recompete for his contract. Other than his signature, the decision-makers didn't know Big Joe. But they knew the hardworking *Rainmaker*. They had come to know the Rainmaker for managing the contract, providing excellent service, and providing outstanding talent to do the work – he was the point of contact for everything.

Before me sat a devastated CEO. When he abdicated his power to the Rainmaker, this fatal mistake left him ignorant about the contracts and operations of his company. Big Joe said his company was spiraling down the drain, and he would have to close its doors in the next six months if he can't find a quick fix. Distressed and feeling helpless, he asked, "how did I let this happened to me?"

If I had asked him, Big Joe probably would have signed a contract with me to save what was left of his company – he was *reactive*. But I wasn't going to let him off the hook so easily. Instead, I asked to spend a few days onsite with him to assess if I wanted to take him on as a client.

Before I start a new project, I learned through my mistakes to do my homework and vet the business owner or CEO to see if they are ready to do the work, or if they merely wanted a band-aid to put on their shit. To have time to learn more about Big Joe and his company, I scheduled a meeting for the next Monday.

In my initial assessment, to see if I wanted to take him on as a client, I collected intel to learn about Big Joe, the company, his leadership team, and how others perceive them. Atlanta is a small town, and the same people meet up at networking events and pre-bid meetings to work their connections to get contracts with local governments. Big contract opportunities everyone pursued were Hartsfield-Jackson Airport, Department of Transportation, CDC, and MARTA. If they were not large enough to prime a contract, the next option was subcontracting for large companies like UJAMMA, H.J. Russell, and the C.D. Moody Company.

The word in many circles was that Big Joe didn't pay his employees fairly and spent a lot of the profits on personal whims, and he was known to be absent for weeks at a time with limited or no communication. Some of his leaders complained about how the company revenue was used as Joe's personal wallet, and they were pissed because they hadn't received a raise in years. Regardless, Joe expected them to work tirelessly to bring in more contracts and make the company look good – *keeping up appearances and bragging rights*. They complained about his profanity, lack of respect, and that he took the employees' loyalty for granted. Some left the company vowing never to work for another black-owned business.

It was known that some of his leaders, including relatives, were disgruntled. If Big Joe was in the office, usually there was a crisis he needed to shut down. During these times, he acted like a CEO, and everyone loved it. They rallied and supported Big Joe to arrest the crisis. My, my, how they admired him. But, as soon as the crisis passed, he went back to his same old shit. He finally paid a price that crippled his company.

As scheduled, I arrived at Anywhere Logistics Solutions at 9:00 a.m. to meet with Big Joe. The receptionist greeted me and escorted me to a conference room and offered me a bottle of water. I asked when Big Joe will arrive? She replied, "He doesn't keep office hours—he comes and goes as he pleases."

After she left the conference room, I walked down a long hallway adorned with the most exquisite black artwork—bold, vibrant abstracts and beautiful portrayal tributes to legendary black entrepreneurs that captured their strength, determination, courage, and success.

The hallway led to an open, sun-kissed loft workplace suited for collaboration, teamwork, and innovative ideas. But it felt like a ghost town—not a soul in a seat, and the phones rang unanswered. The modern designed desks were equipped with the latest technology and gadgets—some looked unused.

I made my way back to the receptionist and asked what time everyone reports to work. She smiled and politely said, "that's not my business."

As I was leaving the receptionist, I heard Big Joe greet her with a flat, "good morning." He showed up for our appointment at 11:00 a.m.—he forgot that we agreed to meet at 9:00. He followed me to the conference room and walked over to an opulent minibar to fix himself a scotch. While he poured the liquor, I packed my briefcase to leave for my next appointment.

Looking surprised, Joe asked, "Where are you going…are you leaving?"

I replied, "I'm going to my next appointment. When you have time to meet, give me a call."

Rushing to block my path to the door, he exclaimed, "Wait! Give me a break!" I simply forgot about our appointment."

With my keys in hand, I walked towards the door. I put my other hand out to shake Big Joe's hand. "Since I don't have any more time to waste, perhaps today is a good day for you to meet with your employees to find out what they do. I'll call you in 30 days."

In a pleading voice, Big Joe said, "I don't know if my company will survive the next 30 days!"

Shaking Joe's hand, I replied, "One thing you can do the next 30 days is to find out what time your employees report to work, and what they do."

And with that, I left.

No Quick Fix

Turning around a company that is teetering on the edge of demise is not a quick fix, nor do I have a magic potion that erases layers of crap instantaneously, as we have come to expect in this digital age.

While Big Joe was meeting with each of his employees, I had more time to do some more digging about his company. He was known as a hustler—streetwise, smooth talker, hungry, and loved to cut a deal, and he started Anywhere Logistics Solutions in 2003. Big Joe idolized Maynard Jackson, who opened doors for black business owners to compete for city and airport contracts. Big Joe got lucky and jumped on Atlanta's black wave—the City prospered under Jackson, and black contractors built profitable businesses that thrive too. Jackson's legacy still influences Atlanta's black entrepreneurs today.

Big Joe was a part of an elite group of black business owners who enjoyed power, success, and influence. At one of their golf events, Big Joe met a contracting officer, who I will call *Sam*. He piqued Big Joe's interest in pursuing federal contracts. Anywhere Logistics Solutions registered to bid and won its first $10 million contract in less than a year. Big Joe couldn't believe the Rainmaker won a big one—he could see how lucrative federal contracts could grow this business.

The company was on a fast growth track, and the trajectory was pointing towards triple-digit profits, positive net gains, and sustainability—Big Joe was doing it, and he became someone you wanted to know. With all of his success, I was intrigued and wanted to know: how did his company end up in the toilet?

In most cases, I get a call when the shit hits the fan, like the one I got from Big Joe. On fewer occasions, I get a call when the business owner or CEO is proactive. They heed the warning signs and take preventive steps to run a solvent business. This type of client is ready and willing to do the work.

Whether a project is proactive or reactive, I start with the why—*why did the company ended up in a downward spiral, and how did they get there? Why did these conditions get so bad, but no one sounded the alarm? Or did a courageous soul indeed sound the alarm, only to have it fall on deaf ears?*

Big Joe was non-committed, but he was desperate for a quick fix. I felt he was trying to hustle me into a deal to put sugar on a pile of shit.

The Messy Truth

There is no short cut to accepting responsibility for the downfall, changing, or a quick fix to your shit—there just isn't! The stink didn't happen all of a sudden, so the cleanup takes time, a plan and a sustainable path for profitable growth.

I recognize we live in a speedy world, but rarely do quick solutions fix fatal mistakes with sustainable results. It takes time to pull back the layers of a company to understand the current state, why it happened, and what it takes to turn around dysfunctional leadership, the culture, and bad financial practices to get to positive returns.

How did Big Joe let his company take a downward spiral?

The answer is a culmination of crap compounded over the years. It became part of the company's norm, and Big Joe stopped minding his business. He was enjoying the benefits of what success afforded him, and he lost sight of disgruntled employees and leadership disengagement. Big Joe also lost sight of himself and why he started his business. Follow the three steps he took to become a great CEO.

STEP I: ACCEPTANCE

Joe didn't wait 30 days to call me. After I left, he called repeatedly, and finally, he got the message that I was not going to take his call. He decided to follow my instructions to meet with his employees to see when they arrived and learn about what they did. Following my instructions, he called me on the 30th day.

"Hello Joe, how are you?"

There was a long silence before he answered. Clearing his throat, he replied, "I am holding on by threads. They are breaking one at a time and slipping through my fingers. *I can't believe my Rainmaker did this to me*—how do I stop this crisis!?"

I didn't express sympathy or empathy but instead redirected his attention to the assignment I asked him to do. "Joe, did you meet with your employees?"

As he spoke, I heard the frustration laced with an assuming undertone in his voice. "Yes, I did, and if I could, I would fire every one of them and start over."

No matter how tough a game Big Joe talked about how he managed the company, the fatal mistakes told a different story. To start, there were no signs of the company or personal accountabilities—starting with him, the CEO. Policies and practices were "loosie goosy" and not in writing. Big Joe blamed everyone except himself—his ego would not allow him to believe anything less than he was a *high roller with a Midas touch.*

His response was not what I expected, but at least he completed the assignment. I asked him: what did you learn from the assignment? Big Joe stated that the management team was not managing the employees—they come and go as they please, no work was getting done, and some left without notice. None of the employees act like they wanted to be at ALS, so it's just a paycheck. Angrily, Big Joe said he paid his managers good money to mind his business.

In response to his venting, I asked Joe if he owned any responsibility for what he observed? Emphatically, he said, "No!" I pay people to do the work. It's not my job to stand over them—that's what I hire the managers to do!"

My questions were a little raw for him, and I wanted him to have time to think about what he learned from the assignment. "Joe, let's schedule another session. I can be there tomorrow at 9:00 a.m. Are there any reasons you can't meet at that time?" I asked. Quickly, he responded no and assured me he would be on time.

I'd hope Big Joe said he accepted responsibility for the current state of circumstances. For some CEOs, accepting their failure is a hard pill to swallow. But if there is going to be change—*sustainable change*—it starts with acceptance. According to a Harvard Business article, the one single behavior that leaders struggle to own is acceptance of their accountability. In other words, *"Do as I say…not as I do."* However, if CEOs want to have a culture of accountability, they must demonstrate and accept the obligation of co-accountability.

When I arrived the following morning, Big Joe was in the lobby to greet me. Standing in front of me, he was dressed in a custom-tailored suit, Gucci shoes, and accessorized with gold jewelry. His face was drawn and tight. Earlier, I found out he needed a loan to make his payroll, and none of his "friends" were willing to spot him $125,000. Just a couple of years ago, he was a man who loved to brag about his money and how his *Midas touch* kept him rolling in the dough.

I asked if we could meet in his war room, which is where the proposal development team mapped out bid-winning strategies, assessed their competitors, and reviewed the final bid documents for submission.

Big Joe hadn't been in the war room in years. His team invited him to be a part of the bid meetings, but he always had something to do or someplace else to be. They wanted his leadership and ideas. His usual response to the team was, "Y'all are the experts…do your *thang*, and win!"

As he walked around the room, he stopped at one of the whiteboards that listed his SMEs (subject matter experts), key personnel, and teaming partners. He looked at one of the matrixes, which outlined a winning strategy for a $45 million contract to provide military support services. He hung his head in despair because the contracting officer was a frat brother. Staring at the opportunity, it was highly likely ALS would have won the contract because *the Rainmaker* had been building a strategy and meeting with his frat brother – the contracting officer – for over a year. In a rage, he smeared the notes to something unrecognizable.

I motioned Big Joe to take a seat. "Why are you angry? Big Joe, if it's not towards yourself, it's misplaced. You are the CEO – everything with ALS begins and ends with you!" In no kind words, I said, "the company is in the toilet because of your ego, neglect and abdicating your authority to the Rainmaker. You created this shit!"

Big Joe looked bewildered and pissed that I dared to speak to him as I did. In a softer tone, I said, "this business depends on you. Until you accept responsibility for your lack of accountability, there is no way up!"

Resigning to his need for help, Big Joe sighed and asked, "Where do we start?

Activity: What are some fatal mistakes you made with your business? _____

_____

_____

_____

_____

_____

How are these mistakes impacting you, your business, and employees? _____

_____

_____

_____

_____

_____

If you are feeling uncomfortable with these questions, your response is similar to that of the CEOs and business owners I've coached. When your company is on the brink of demise, my job is to help you make the right decisions to begin the turn-around. Additionally, when your fatal mistakes cloud your thinking, decision-making is impaired by the following reactions:

- **Exaggerated pride or self-confidence**, which causes you to ignore information and insight from other resources. You convince yourself that the status quo will fix the problem, and "stick-and-stay" is the way forward.
- **Anger**, which is appeased with a bunch of excuses, or anger misdirected at your leaders instead of yourself.
- **Short-sightedness**, which impairs your ability to see the future consequence of your mistakes.
- **Paralysis**, which is consumed by self-pity, or no awareness that your next decision may be reactionary, and likely to be another fatal mistake.

Big Joe had experienced all four reactions, but this is not the end of his story – it's the beginning of an introspective experience that uncovered the shit he created. I hope you take this journey with Joe and learn from his fatal mistakes.

> A man must be big enough to admit his mistakes, smart enough to profit from them, and strong enough to correct them.
>
> **John C. Maxwell, CEO**

Before we started, I asked Big Joe to agree that he will do the following things for us to fix the problems:

1. Accept responsibility for the demise of the company
2. Get a grip on the current situation
3. Plan to address all stakeholders – investors, employees, suppliers, creditors, and customers

4. Evaluate the company and be willing to change – examine core
    business, capital, culture, talent, and resources

Reluctantly, Big Joe extended his hand to solidify our agreement.
"Oh, by the way, bring your A-game," I said with a smile. Understandably,
he was not in a cordial mood. This session was exhausting mentally, and
we both needed time to reflect and think about a path forward.

THE RAINMAKER

The Capital Spot was buzzing with the latest news about a new contract for logistics services for a local military base. As the Rainmaker finished his lunch and shut down his laptop, Big Joe slid into the booth seat across from him.

"I'm a little surprised to see you," the Rainmaker said. "Usually, you're on one of your global treks. What happened...did you run out of money?" As he slid out of his seat to stand up, Big Joe grabbed his arm. The Rainmaker stood rigid in the tight aisle while people hustled past him. A few men and associates who knew both men watched the contact. The word on the street was that the Rainmaker had decided he'd had enough of Big Joe and decided to set up his own company and use his contacts and connections for himself.

Big Joe let his hand linger. "Look man, I'm not here to cause a scene," he told the Rainmaker as he leaned forward over the table. "Not here, but meet me at the cigar room for a private conversation."

The Rainmaker felt a wrenching in his chest. "How dare you!" He felt his forehead tighten. Snatching his arm away, he told Big Joe, "I don't take orders from you anymore!"

Looking confused, Big Joe asked, "Man, what in the world did I do that caused you to stab me in the back?"

"Ha! Stab you in the back!?" The Rainmaker loosened his tie to relieve the restricting collar around his neck. "How many times did you stab me in the back and keep your foot on my neck? How many times did you take advantage of the employees? How many times did you say thank you to your team who kept your the business going while you were off traveling the world…stab *you* in the back!?"

Big Joe didn't like the Rainmaker's tone and boldness to confront him. "Man, keep your voice down. We don't need to tell our business here," Big Joe uttered a deep guttural sound.

The Rainmaker shook his head. "I don't care if people know about your shit. Why ain't you bragging now, *High Roller*?"

Still seated, Big Joe looked around, and a few so-called friends in his elite circle watched and listened to Rainmaker confronting him. He wanted to walk away, but the Rainmaker blocked the aisle in front of him, and people were standing in the aisle behind him. Big Joe could hear their whispers and gasps of shock.

The Rainmaker loathed every time one of Big Joe's elite friends said how he called him his *golden goose* and bragged about how he kept his foot on his neck to make sure he laid golden eggs – it was humiliating!

The Rainmaker felt his throat tighten again as he looked down at his old boss. "Big Joe, I don't owe you anything. I decided I was tired of being disrespected, humiliated, working hard to build your business, and barely making enough to take care of my family. I was with you day one when you started your company. You can find money to indulge your whims, but you can't find a dime to give your employees a raise – some of them have to get food stamps to make ends meet. I don't owe you anything," said the Rainmaker as he straightened up and backed away from the booth.

Before the Rainmaker turned to walk towards the door, he reached into his wallet to pull a business card. He tossed it on the table in front of Big Joe. "I'm done with you – here's my attorney's information. Call him to contact me."

Feeling convicted by the Rainmaker's words, Big Joe reached for the card Rainmaker tossed on the table. He had no idea the Rainmaker despised him. As Big Joe recalled times he berated the Rainmaker, he believed he had good reasons. Big Joe thought he treated the Rainmaker like his right-hand man, and he depended on the Rainmaker to run his company. *"Where did I go wrong?"*

STEP II: A CATALYST
FOR CHANGE

The following afternoon, Big Joe and I met again in his war room. Clearing away clutter from a stylish silver chrome and glass Benhar conference table, we outlined a short list of action items. I told him about my plan to fix his company in 120 days. My plan included the following steps:

- Start with the why – Why did he want to be a business owner?
- Chart a timeline of past growth and warning signs of decline
- Identify why the company went into decline
- Identify his role in the decline of the company
- Assess his leadership style and what needs to change
- Help him decide what kind of company he wants to be
- Decide what type of CEO he wants to be
- Create a turnaround plan – identify obstacles and actions to move forward
- With his team, develop a 120-day repair plan and new three-year strategic plans

- Identify the business core values
- Review the financials and current cash flow
- Review the necessity for leadership and his support to their success
- Schedule a "State of the Business Address" to communicate his strategy to save the company
- Establish milestones to measure results and sustainability

As his company hung in the balance of surviving, Big Joe conceded that he made a few mistakes and checked his ego. The contact with the Rainmaker found its way to his conscious, and the rebuke made Big Joe more pliable to listen and receive feedback.

"Joe, you seem distracted. If you are not all in, let's not waste time," I said. Quietly and sounding wounded, he said he wanted to move forward to save his company.

Surprisingly, he gave in to letting me take the lead. I expected several rounds of deflecting, blaming, and denying how the company got in this downward spiral. Instead, he let go of all his excuses and accepted responsibility – *he was ready to do the work.*

Another thought that distracted Big Joe was that none of his "so-called" friends came to stand by him while the Rainmaker criticized him. They all looked on, and their silence essentially condoned the Rainmaker's rebuke.

Before we ended our session, Big Joe mentioned the contact with the Rainmaker. "Sounds like it didn't go so well – what did you expect," I asked?

"I've never seen the Rainmaker angry or ever raise his voice – he cursed me. He sounded like I hurt him," said Big Joe.

Debilitating Mindsets

One thing I know for sure – all failing businesses have failing owners or CEOs, poor management, and are unwilling to change. Denial is mixed with excuses and refusal to accept responsibility. Only when you are willing to examine fatal mistakes and replace old behaviors with new ones will possibilities happen to help take your company out of a dire situation.

Secondly, all failing businesses have owners or CEOs who are consumed by one or more of these issues:

1. Fear of taking a risk, listening to new ideas or losing control	2. An ego that goes unchecked and interferes with building healthy relationships with employees and customers
3. A belief that you don't need great talent and resources to succeed	4. A lack of priorities, with a belief they don't have enough time to manage the business
5. A lack of confidence	6. A belief that current circumstances necessitate the decisions made, and an expectation for others to believe the same

Activity: Of the six issues, which do you think Big Joe is most consumed with?_____

_____

_____

_____

Question: Of the six issues, which are you most consumed?

_____

_____

_____

What is one action step you can take to improve to correct the issue? _____

_____

_____

_____

_____

What Is Your WHY?

Back in the day, many farmers, sharecroppers, as well as displaced professionals during the Civil Rights movement started a business because it was a way to survive. Today, Black entrepreneurs have a different perspective and experience. Here are a few answers I've heard from clients and entrepreneurs:

- I'm a lousy employee
- I wanted to help people who walked in my shoes
- I wanted to do and share what I love
- I believed I could accomplish my goals and be an inspiration to others
- I wanted my freedom and independence

There are many reasons why people want to be a business owner, and the core of our choice is freedom – to make a difference, how we commit our time and have the freedom to earn money.

Sometimes, when we have an idea to start a business, our "WHY" has not crystalized. As you execute your business plan and develop your company, your vision revolves around a set of targets and standards. And while the freedom of not having anyone standing over you is exciting, the stress of knowing you bear the responsibilities of failures can drive you or defeat you. It is vital to know your "why."

Question: What is your "WHY" and how did you come to know it is your why?_____

_____

_____

_____

_____

_____

Question: When you decided to be a business owner, what kind of business did you aspire to have? _____

_____

_____

_____

_____

_____

What kind of CEO did you aspire to be?_____

_____

_____

_____

_____

_____

Big Joe also has a "WHY", and the next phase is to take him through a series of exercises to help him reconnect with his noble reason.

THE PRINCIPLES OF CHANGE

"Why did you want to be an entrepreneur?" I asked. Standing up, Big Joe paced and circled the room a couple of times before he spoke.

"My father was a janitor at a Jewish grocery store, and Mr. Ezra, who owned the store, took an interest in me. I went to the store after school to help my father clean up, but Mr. Ezra stopped me from helping my dad. He liked me. The Jew took me everywhere – meetings, the bank, and to buy big pallets of food and goods for the store. He also took me with him when he dropped off groceries to poor people or went to the old folk homes. One day, Mr. Ezra told me, "Joe, your papa is a good man and a hard worker. You need to make him proud. Son, you can own your own business."

Looking around his war room, Joe said, "I wanted to be a business owner so I could give people jobs, help my community, and make my father proud – I wanted to be a millionaire."

"Joe, those are all great reasons for wanting to be a business owner," I said. I was beginning to feel hopeful that I could help him repair his company. In this session, Big Joe would discover what it takes to reconnect with his "WHY," and how to get there.

One of my methods of establishing a baseline is to gauge his interest and willingness to do the work. "Joe, the next step is to measure how invested you are to lead your company to a future state that you desire. "

"I know that if I want my company to survive, I need to take responsibility to lead the change, but I've never done anything like this, and I'm not confident that I can lead my company through this process. I see the benefits, but I don't have the talent," said Big Joe. From a deck of playing cards on the table, he pulled out a seven of diamonds to indicate his level of willingness and interest to do the work. He doubted his capabilities.

Activity: On a scale of 1-10, how much are you willing to do the work? _____

Explain why you chose that number. _____

_____

_____

_____

_____

"Joe, I'm glad to see you are beginning to come around. Seven is a good place to start. Are you ready to learn more about how you can save your company?" I asked. He followed me, and sat at the other side of the table with a pad and pencil.

The process of taking an organization that is in the toilet or has started a descent is step-by-step. BHFL's winning strategy involves these ten principles for change to be successful:

1. ***Culture is everything***. It is more than a buzzword. Successful leaders understand that culture is more important than any system. Culture is the common belief held by every leader and is taught to every employee. It is a unique differentiator that separates your company from any other organization. I coined culture as "this is how we do it."

   For culture to transform into a new state to achieve desired changes, we manage the fear of and resistance to change. As humans, our brain creates routines and habits, and we become stuck in our ways and unwilling to consider thinking of or doing something different. When done right, it's incredible to see it in action. The company's values and beliefs are demonstrated in job satisfaction, engagement, integrity, productivity, drive, and ultimately success.

2. **TBSH – The Buck Stops Here.** Before starting the transformation phase, it is imperative that the CEO is involved and supports his executive leaders and the planning phase. We start this step by examining what's in place: the company's strategic plan. We facilitate the planning at an off-site meeting to begin a rigorous exercise to explore the organization's current state, the transitional phase, and the desired future state. The activity includes an assessment that reveals the leadership team's strengths and gaps, a communication strategy to launch the project, and critical milestones to measure progress. During this step, we also facilitate an opportunity for the executive leaders to align and adopt our model for success. Each executive gives a presentation to illustrate his or her role to support successful outcomes.

3. **Inclusive of Everyone.** I've seen so many times the executive leadership team decides to make major changes without involving

middle management and all employees. This approach is expensive, with a minimum, if any, return on investment. This step is vital to communicate the change and minimize sabotage efforts to maintain the status quo. The effort to be inclusive about rolling out change is immeasurably more productive. It gains traction when middle management and key frontline employees are engaged early to provide insight and input on possible issues that may be obstacles.

4. **Make the Case for Change – WIIFM (what's in it for me).** Most change initiatives are a nightmare and unsuccessful because leadership communicates a business model to improve market share or growth for the company. Employees simply do not care about this. To be successful, the message must deliver clear benefits to make it palatable and easy to understand in a way that matters to them.

5. **Demonstrate the Change You Want to Achieve.** I won't tell you how many failed change initiatives did not achieve target outcomes because the CEO and his executive team assumed that by merely saying it, the change would happen—poof! Nor can you depend on PowerPoint presentations, charts, and graphs to make the emotional connection needed to make the change. The CEO and executive leaders must visibly come out of their comfort zone to model new behaviors the employee will believe. It starts at the top – be the example you want to achieve.

6. E^3 -- **Engage, Engage, Engage.** As you are starting to see, communication is a common denominator. CEOs often make a mistake assuming that change begins with their endorsement, holding a few meetings, and people will know what to do. Nothing is further from the truth. Meaningful and lasting change requires consistent and frequent communication, starting

with the WHY and throughout each phase of the initiative. Communication and messaging can be enforced with signs – involve employees and teams to create posters and engage everyone to participate. Have a little fun and friendly competition.

7. **Deploy Special Teams.** Our model trains each level of the organization to learn a five-step process, and we facilitate the selection of special teams to cascade the principles down through the company. These teams are ambassadors for change, and they galvanize engagement and buy-in so that change is adopted and sustained throughout the organization. The role of the special teams is to influence, motivate, and recognize peers or anyone in their group who demonstrate the desired behavior or innovates an outdated process with a modern approach. Encourage the ambassadors to showcase accolades for their group – create a spotlight that everyone can share.

8. **Hire an Expert.** The information I share is a good starting point, but if your business is in the toilet, and you are part of the cause, you need to hire an expert. BHFL Group is a certified practitioner, and we help organizations achieve success by maximizing the goals of the business objectives, deploying change strategies across the organization, and increasing capabilities and capacity. The skills of a certified practitioner include the following competencies:
   a. Interpersonal/Teambuilding
   b. Project Management
   c. Communication Skills
   d. Problem Solving
   e. Training & Development
   f. Presentation Skills

    g. Multitasking (Ability to work on multiple deliverables or projects at once)

    h. Business Acumen

    i. Facilitation

    j. Coaching

    k. Clarify/Simplify Complex Problems

9. **Use Creative, Informal Solutions.** When establishing a new culture, change can easily be undermined by people returning to old behaviors. Using such tools as a leaderboard, metrics, or a thermometer to monitor and communicate progress is a simple way to reinforce and sustain goals achieved. Slogans such as, "On time, Every time" is a simple way to incorporate a standard with a new norm. We also offer a train-the-trainer program to develop managers to be coaches. Coaching is an informal approach to help employees overcome obstacles or resistance that impacts buy-in and engagement.

10. **MMRM – Measure, Maintain, Reinforce & Measure.** Whatever you do, don't let your hard work and all that you accomplish relapse. We've been called to help organizations who failed to measure, reinforce, and maintain the change. Failure to do these three steps deprives the organization of a sense of accomplishment and opens the door to return to old behaviors. It is imperative to reinforce the new norms to sustain and maintain a trajectory that points up.

The results Big Joe wants to achieve are not only for him – this process encompasses the whole organization. His current employees and leaders will also need to change. Part of Joe's success also depends on changing current attitudes, behaviors, and beliefs to adopt new ones to be more productive.

Activity: Based on Big Joe's story, what is one reason for him to change? _____

_____

_____

_____

For the employees, what is one reason for them to be a part of the change?_____

_____

_____

_____

What is one reason for you to change? _____

_____

_____

_____

For your employees, what is one reason for them to be a part of the change?_____

_____

_____

_____

STEP III: CREATE A NEW NORM

Change is possible when leaders and employees find new ways to be as individuals, teams, and discover new ways to work. When Big Joe, his leaders, and his employees collectively want to change the current state, find a better way to interact, communicate and work, these building blocks become the footstone to build a culture that benefits everyone.

To start this process, Big Joe and I reviewed the steps to assess the current state (what needs to be fixed), plan for the transition (how to get there), and execute the project (do the work) to achieve the desired future state of the organization.

Although Big Joe's fatal mistakes are about him, the impact of these mistakes went well beyond him. For a successful turnaround, BHFL's approach assesses stakeholders impacted by the fatal mistakes, identifies roll-out obstacles, creates comprehensive change plans, and establishes benchmarks or metrics to track the impact of change results.

Below is BHFL's 120-day plan for fixing fatal mistakes and setting a new direction to turn around a company:

Phase	Description	Tool & Exercise
Week 1	Preparation for Change	The Five Stages of Change and Start with Your Personal "WHY"
Week 2	Present Personal & Business Model for Change	Self-Assessment – Personal Awareness, Desire to Change, Knowledge on How to Change, Ability to acquire new behaviors and skills to change.
Week 3 & 4	Readiness to Change	Assess Individual Readiness to Adopt Change – Why the Company Needs to Change. Examine: (1) Current State (2) Transitional Phase (3) Future State
Week 5	Establish Transitional Training and Communication Plan	Start with a Framework. Identify What Needs to Change and What Company/Individuals Behaviors to Change. Implement the required skills and behaviors.
Week 6	Assess Talent Gaps	Identify talent needs, gaps, and misalignment. Evaluate corporate culture and establish a talent team advisory committee
Week 7	Hold Town Hall Meeting	Communicate Personal Accountability to Change, & Review the Plan

Phase	Description	Tool & Exercise
Week 8	Complete Core Value & Strength-Based Assessments	Identify business core values and employees' strengths
Week 9 & 10	Develop customized leadership and teambuilding training	Develop and communicate leadership and team training schedule
Week 11 & 12	Assign leadership and team projects	Provide each team an assignment to present to achieve target goals and outcomes
Week 13 & 14	Develop milestones, key performance indicators, and metrics to track	Project SME collects data and creates leaderboards or kiosk to display
Week 15	Plan for Celebration & Spotlight Management, Employees' Individual and Team Initiatives	Deploy a special team to organize the celebration
Week 16	Wrap-up & Celebration	Presentation to review the "WHY," Accomplishments and Steps to Maintain End Project with Celebration!

Obstacles to Starting the Change

Big Joe unbuttoned his shirt collar and tugged at the neck of his shirt. "Coach, I want to take this leap, but I don't think I can right now. My company is ruined, and I can't find enough money to make payroll – what's the purpose of this turn-around plan? I won't have a company in 120 days," he said.

To address his immediate need, I asked Big Joe to call his executive assistant to join us. His assistant was Ms. Sarah, and she had been with Big Joe for over ten years. She started as a temp, and she still worked as a temp.

She was an older woman and was a very poised, talented assistant. Clearing her throat, she asked, "Mr. Joe, how can I help you?" He looked at me to answer her question. I asked Ms. Sarah what she knew about accounting and the company's bank accounts. She left the room and brought back several files. Big Joe learned that Ms. Sarah had made copies of the bank statements before she gave them to the Rainmaker. Joe was shocked to learn there was a second bank account set up as a reserve fund because the Rainmaker could not control his spending. In the second bank account, it had a positive balance of $500,000 in reserve.

Feeling relieved to know that he could make payroll, Big Joe became excited and felt hopeful he could save his company.

Activity: What is an obstacle(s) that is a barrier for you to start your change? _____

_____

_____

_____

Seven Fatal Mistakes that Defeats Change

There are many reasons why business owners fail, but the seven fatal mistakes I train and coach my clients to avoid are:

1. Failure to be accountable
2. Failure to be visible and engaged
3. Failure to keep their ego in check
4. Failure to share the spotlight
5. Inability to communicate inclusively
6. Failure to listen, clarify and implement the mission and direction
7. Failure to invest in their professional development

Failure to Be Accountable

One of the perks of being a business owner is freedom. You are the absolute decision-maker, and the course you chart for the company rests in your hands. But freedom is also a double-edged sword: As the CEO, there is no one to hold you accountable, which without any boundaries, may ultimately lead to an unhappy team. To give your company a path upward, implement a system of checks and balances that ensures your leaders are heard and considered when you make decisions that impact the entire business.

Failure to be Visible and Engaged

We all hear how lonely it is at the top – but is this true? Or, are you suffering from "invisible CEO syndrome?" Are you missing in action or just out of sight?

Visibility is essential to leadership and employee engagement. One of my mentors told me years ago, *"It's hard to lead from behind a desk."* Every morning, I left the safety of my office to make it a routine to do my rounds, and I attended key meetings for visibility and contributed to solutions to solve complex issues.

Failure to Keep Ego in Check

We all have succumbed to our ego – some more than others. Some CEOs' success inflates their ego so much so that it makes them manipulative – it dulls their concern for others and corrupts their behavior, often causing them to go against their values and morals. In other words, the more successful we are as entrepreneurs, the more at risk we are of getting an inflated ego. And, the bigger the ego grows, the more likely we become an insulated bubble, losing touch with your employees, the mission, and ultimately the clients – *power blinds reality.*

Instead of being surrounded by people who speak the truth, I have seen it so often how CEOs surround themselves with people who speak to their ego – "yes" people. I read a quote Bill Gates famously said, "Success is a lousy teacher. It seduces smart people into thinking they can't lose."

Also, what does your swag say about you – "look at me!" Without a check on the ego, it is likely to lead to substantial consequences, including being surrounded by people who don't add value and are willing to do wrong things to please you.

Finally, an unchecked ego causes disillusion and twist your values. This is important to remember because our behavior is affected by perceived truths. One of my favorite movies, *Shaka Zulu,* illustrates this point. He was a mighty warrior who revolutionized warfare and built the Zulu kingdom. As he became more powerful, he believed he was invisible and became more brutal, ruthless, and bizarre. He used his power for revenge, and the Zulu Empire grew to more than 250,000, one of the largest empires in the history of Southern Africa – he was a builder who became a destroyer.

Failure to Share the Spotlight

Success and power are intoxicating, and some CEOs seek the spotlight. They hunger for the spotlight, they want to stay in the spotlight, and they forget to shine the spotlight on others. Two of my favorite books are *Servant Leadership* and *Leading from Behind*.

The philosophy behind Servant Leadership is a set of practices that enrich the lives of individuals, build better organizations, and ultimately create a more inclusive community. A measure of your share is this: are the people you serve thriving or dying?

Do you set a standard to nourish, support, and foster growth and development? Are your employees becoming healthier, smarter, more self-sufficient, better-performing, and effective team players? What you give to your employees is what they will to your customers and how they will help each other.

According to a Harvard Review article, the most effective leaders will lead from behind. Nelson Madella likens leadership to a shepherd, "He stays behind the flock, letting the most nimble go out ahead, where upon the others follow, not realizing that all along they are being directed from behind."

Employees are looking for more meaning and purpose at work. The best way to retain your talent is to show respect and value their contribution to the success of the company. Employees want to add their footprint to the organization's purpose. They want to be a part of a company that serves their local communities.

Failure to Invest in their Professional Development

Whether you are a business owner or start-up entrepreneur, leading and developing a company is a daunting task. Ironically, some of the fatal mistakes are caused by a much more basic failure—the failure of CEOs to invest in their leadership, capabilities, and staying abreast of emerging technologies or business trends.

Also, CEOs or business owners who have forgotten how to lead themselves are generally at risk for committing fatal mistakes or exhibiting personal behaviors that end up in the news. Their organizations could end up in the toilet, and they fail to realize the need to engage in continuous self-awareness to hone their leadership capabilities and mitigate such risks.

Activity: Self-Evaluation

On a scale of 1 (the lowest) to 3 (the highest), rate your behaviors and write how you can change/improve the behavior on the following items:

The Behavior	Your Score	The Change
How well do you hold yourself accountable?		
To what degree are you visible and engaged with your leaders and employees?		

The Behavior	Your Score	The Change
How well do you keep your ego in check		
How well do you share the spotlight with other achievers in your organization?		
How well do you communicate inclusively – with your leaders and all employees?		
How well do you listen, clarify and implement the mission, and give direction?		
How much do you invest in training your leadership and personal development?		

To finish this exercise, complete this sentence:

I want to become a better business owner. I am committed to

_____

_____

> He who rejects change is the architect of decay
>
> **Harold Wilson**

I left Big Joe to do this exercise on his own. As we talked about the six fatal mistakes, a few times, he seemed conflicted and attempted to deny that he committed any of the fatal mistakes.

The first time I did this exercise myself, in a 3-day leadership lock-in session, it was raw and debilitating to acknowledge that I committed some of these fatal mistakes. But if I wanted to improve, it was essential to identify my missteps, accept them, and do the work to become a better leader.

When I returned to the war room, Leech and Big Joe were celebrating with high-5s and a scotch. "What are you two celebrating?" I asked. Leech turned on the CD player and did a breakdance move. "We ain't in trouble no more. We got money in the bank!" he said. Big Joe urged him on as he sipped his liquor.

Since Leech interrupted our session, I told Big Joe we were at a good stopping point. "Joe, you are on the path to saving your company. I will send you a schedule for us to review," I said.

Before I left, I wanted Joe to be prepared to start our meeting by sharing his findings from the initial exercise to meet with his employees and find out what they do. "Joe, let's take a closer look at your employees' meetings when I return tomorrow. I think there's more than your comments," I said.

Leech and Big Joe were busy celebrating their sudden windfall. Big Joe didn't hear me. My request fell on deaf ears, drowned out by Leech's rapping to the music.

I was concerned by the interaction I observed between Big Joe and Leech. My intel source told me Leech was Big Joe's nephew, and he'd been with the company for about five years. Leech was described as someone unwilling to participate in the work to find better solutions but very willing to take more than his fair share of rewards. Big Joe liked him because he was agreeable, edgy, and easy to be around. Big Joe kept Leech around because he kept him informed when he was away. Leech was a yes-man – Leech said what Big Joe wanted to hear.

THE LEECH

Since Big Joe's good fortune, he had been expected to take care of the family and obligated by the family elders. He also liked to brag at the annual reunions that it was he alone who bankrolled the family – new homes, mink coats, vacations, and jobs. At one of the yearly reunions, he showed a slide show about all the things he endowed the family. To stay in his good grace, some relatives faked their gratitude for his goodwill. They talked among themselves about the *gift of entitlement* and joked about how easy it was to stroke Big Joe's ego.

Leech mastered the art of getting anything he wanted from Big Joe. His mama, Big Joe's aunt, called him one day and begged Big Joe to give Leech a job. She was tired of Leech loafing around on her dime.

On his first day, Leech arrived to work after lunch. Big Joe was out of town, and the Rainmaker didn't know anything about a new employee being hired. Leech made sure everyone knew he was Big Joe's nephew.

Leech felt entitled. The other employees described him as a parasite, which sucks the lifeblood out of the company. He was unfriendly and seldom volunteered or participated in team projects. He was also known as a snitch and kept Big Joe informed when he was out of the office. His only concern was getting a paycheck.

Activity: Do you have leeches in your organization?

_____

How do you handle entitled relatives and friends who work for you?_____

_____

_____

_____

_____

_____

_____

False Impressions

When I arrived the following morning, Big Joe was in a different mood. "Joe, how are you doing this morning?" I asked. As though he needed time to gather his thoughts and choose his words, he asked to meet in his office, which was located at the other end of the loft.

As we sat down at his small conference table, he blurted out, "Hey, you know what? I am not convinced I need to make any of the changes we talked about yesterday. I believe I can do this on my own. The key thing is I have the reserve fund to work with, and the other thing I need to do is to hire more people to replace the ones who left with the Rainmaker," he said.

"Joe," I said, "I think the reserve fund has changed your viewpoint on turning the company around. When you called me, you said your company was spiraling down the drain, and you would have to close its doors within six months. You were distressed and felt helpless."

"Well, I realized that all I need to do is keep my payroll going, win another contract, and hire a new team. I've been in tough spots before and have always been able to pull myself up," said Big Joe as he tried to convince himself he had all the answers.

"Ok, let's look at your talent. What did you find out in your meetings? How many employees do you currently have?"

Joe opened a spreadsheet. He listed the following positions remaining:

- 1 Executive Assistant
- 1 Receptionist
- 6 Administrative Assistants
- 4 Inbound Call Technicians
- 2 Project Managers
- 3 Supervisors
- 4 Managers
- 1 Director
- 1 Vice President

Big Joe sorted the employees into the following categories – administrative support, managers, and leaders. He summarized each group as follows:

Administrative Staff – skills are limited, minimum productivity, and none are superstars, except one. His Executive Assistant, Ms. Sarah, was a hard worker, anticipated problems, and initiated solutions.

Tech Support – Including Leech, the team spends most of their time surfing the web, playing video games, and joking around with each other. Calls stay in the queue too long, leading customers to drop the calls.

People Leaders (Managers & Supervisors) – They have no ideas or any solutions to move the company forward. They are unclear about their roles and seldom communicate with their employees. They stay in their offices and rarely offer direction or prioritize the work to be done.

Senior Leaders (Vice President & Director) – Both are in the marketing department and seldom are in the office. When they are in the office, much of their time is spent reading magazines, on the Internet, and conference calls. Neither of them asked questions about the Rainmaker and what happened to the company.

As Big Joe read his notes, his mood shifted to be more subdued. "How did they interact with you?" I asked.

Visibly uncomfortable with my question, Big Joe said some asked why he was there, some were angry and told him he didn't care about the company or what happened to them, and many of them asked how long he planned to be there. He got up from his desk and walked to the window and stared at the skyline. The silence was deafening. Joe was a stranger to his own company.

> A point of view can be a dangerous luxury when substituted for insight and understanding.
>
> **Marshall McLuhan**

Activity: Earlier, I listed seven fatal mistakes that defeat change. Review Joe's Self-Assessment and write one recommendation to help him to become more self-aware.

Rating Scale: 1 (the lowest) to 3 (the highest)

The Behavior	Rating	The Change
How well do you hold yourself accountable?	3	I depend on the executive team to do what it takes to grow the business. I keep them accountable.
To what degree are you visible and engaged with your leaders and employees?	1	I don't need to be visible – I pay my managers to supervise their employees. They see me when I am in the office.
How well do you keep your ego in check	3	I have a healthy ego and confidence.
How well do you share the spotlight with other achievers in your organization?	1	Only the company spoke person is in the spotlight. I am responsible for this role.

Based on Big Joe's self-assessment, what are your recommendations to help him to address fatal mistakes that defeat change? _____

_____

_____

_____

_____

_____

_____

Get it Right!

Big Joe was conflicted and teetering on the fence between believing he can solve the problem and denying there is one.

The success of change relies on Big Joe's acceptance and commitment to the need to change. If he is not clear about the need to change, how would he convince employees who resist change, and those employees have positive and negative feelings about change? Who among his current employees could be influential to the resisters and those ambivalent about adopting the initiative?

After some time looking out of his 25th-floor window, Big Joe thought about Leech, the meetings with the employees, and how he lost sight of his company, and the signs that warned of his fatal mistakes.

It's not uncommon to see CEOs waver and look for an exit out of situations that spotlight their faults or responsibility for the company's decline. The common problem is that we give in to short-sighted behaviors and habits, and sometimes we can't see how misguided these behaviors are.

Activity: Explain how Big Joe is being short-sighted about the needs of the business._____

_____

_____

_____

_____

_____

_____

Describe a difficult situation you faced about your business, and what things you did that were short-sighted.

_____

_____

_____

_____

_____

_____

How did these behaviors and habits impact your role in fixing your fatal mistakes?_____

_____

_____

_____

_____

Big Joe contemplated the state of his company and whether he could pick up the ruins and make the repairs himself. He was at a crossroad.

"I thought about the cash reserve and my comments to do this on my own. Leech is my nephew, and I just realized how he could sidetrack me."

"Joe, Leech is a 'yes-man.' What could be a different reaction to him when he applauds and encourages you to act on an impulsive idea? As well as you know him, is Leech a deficit to the company who cares more about himself vs. the good of the entire company? I think this issue is a good problem and will help you to prepare to make some tough decisions ahead."

"I agree that I was impulsive and got caught up in the moment of having the reserve fund that relieved my concerns. I got caught up in listening to Leech telling me that my problem was fixed, I got side-tracked." As Big Joe walked away from the window, he appeared more thoughtful about his behavior and how easily he was blindsided – this could have been another fatal mistake.

"Coach, let's stick to the plan and move forward." As we ended the session, Joe was tasked with three assignments:

- Make a list of "yes" people who, in the past, have influenced his decisions
- Chart a timeline of past growth and warning signs of decline
- Identify why the company went into decline

Activity: "Yes," people are those who speak to your ego and seldom tell you the truth. They always agree with you and want to please you. "Yes" people tell you what you want to hear and rarely give constructive feedback.

Who are some "yes" people you go to for advice?

_____

_____

_____

_____

_____

How do you check the advice you receive from a "yes" person?

_____

_____

_____

_____

_____

How can "yes" people defeat change?_____

_____

_____

_____

_____

The next session will drill down further into the company and explore the next steps towards create a turnaround plan.

DO THE WORK

Instead of our usual routine meeting, I asked Big Joe to meet at my office. I made arrangements with another CEO client and his team to have Big Joe observe their change initiative to introduce a new product to the market. The meeting focused on their talent readiness assessment and identified gaps that could hinder a successful launch. I also wanted Big Joe to see a possible outcome he could achieve by committing to doing the work. As I prepared him for the next phase – a transitional plan – Big Joe would need to assess his company for the turn-around as he prepared for his company's first town hall meeting.

Surprisingly, Big Joe arrived 15 minutes before our meeting. Instead of his custom made suit, Big Joe was dressed down in a crisp white shirt and dress slacks. I noticed that no diamond rings and braces adorned his outfit. Instead of his Gucci leather loafers, he wore a pair of well worn black, lace-up dress shoes.

"Good morning Joe," I said as I fixed a cup of tea. He nodded his head and took a seat at the T-shape table. He opened his notepad to ready himself for our meeting. "I have a surprise for you," I said to Big Joe as I sat down at the head of the table. "I think it will be helpful for you to observe a talent readiness assessment meeting I am facilitating with a CEO client and his team. They are launching a new product," I said.

"If it helps me to turn my company around, I'm open to learning what I should have been doing all along if I had minded my business," said Joe. I was a little surprised by Big Joe's comment. "Joe, I'm impressed and appreciate that you are becoming more open-minded to thinking differently," I said. "Let walk over to the think tank." Trailing behind me, Big Joe asked, "what is a think-tank?" Before I could answer, my client, Mr. Seller, came over to shake my hand, and then he took a seat with his team. On the wall facing the door was a slogan: "Better Thinking for Better Results."

There are many meanings for the word "Think Tank." Still, I use it to describe how I work with my clients and to invite diverse thinking styles towards solving problems and finding solutions that take into consideration the business and the customer, using diverse people and ideas. In the middle of the room were rolling desks surrounded by wall-to-wall whiteboards, colorful markers, Post-it notepads, laptops, and a printer.

Mr. Seller kicked-off the team meeting and stated the outcomes for the team readiness assessment – evaluate key leaders and employees for six characteristics to prepare for a successful project launch.

When Mr. Seller and I completed the readiness assessment, he and his leadership team discovered key gaps in six characteristics. To close the gaps, the entire team participated in mapping out solutions and timelines with color codes on the whiteboard. Once they finished the exercise, the plan was captured to paper and printed.

A few times, I was able to catch a glimpse of Big Joe taking notes and being attentive to the process. At the end of the session, Big Joe asked Mr. Seller questions about the exercise and its benefits.

"Joe, I was on the brink of losing my company because I let the company become a dinosaur in the modern world. I was afraid to try new concepts, ideas, or trust my leaders. The experience was humbling, but I saved my

company. We are two years into our strategic plan and back in the black."
After Mr. Seller left, Big Joe and I returned to my office to start his session.

"Let's dive into the agenda for the meeting," I said to Big Joe. He was deep in thought. "A penny for your thoughts," I said.

"Coach, I think I can do this. It's not a quick fix, but I'm beginning to see a way up." Big Joe took a deep breath and said, "I'm ready."

Joe took out the list of employees and his notes. To help him with the exercise, I drew a readiness assessment grid on the whiteboard.

"Joe, using this assessment tool, I want you to use the information you gathered during your 1:1 meetings to rank your employees. The scale is one (1) as the lowest, and ten (10) is the highest. Once you rate the employees, the next step is to circle the scores that are five or higher.

Employee Readiness Assessment

Employee Name	Attribute	Rating
Executive Assistant		
	Learning & Development	8
	Service & Quality Focus	8
	Engagement	6
	Job Performance	8
	Company Confidence	6
	Teamwork	9
Project Manager		
	Learning & Development	4
	Service & Quality Focus	5
	Engagement	5
	Job Performance	4
	Company Confidence	2
	Teamwork	4
Leech		
	Learning & Development	3
	Service & Quality Focus	4
	Engagement	4
	Job Performance	3
	Company Confidence	8
	Teamwork	4
Supervisor		
	Learning & Development	6
	Service & Quality Focus	6
	Engagement	7
	Job Performance	5
	Company Confidence	3
	Teamwork	4
Director		
	Learning & Development	3
	Service & Quality Focus	4
	Engagement	2
	Job Performance	4
	Company Confidence	4
	Teamwork	4

As he looked at the results, Big Joe felt a level of anxiety as he surveyed the employees' overall readiness ratings – only one employee in this group ranked high in all categories, and two other employees had some scores ranked at least a five. Leech and his most senior leader ratings were the worst.

Big Joe looked at the results and wondered how he was going to rebuild the company with the talent he has. Standing back from the board, he studied the numbers. "This is my fault, and I have to fix it."

Big Joe never gave two thoughts to how important his employees' talent was to his success. As he recalled his 1:1 conversations, the ratings mean a lot more than his disappointment and frustrations. Big Joe was beginning to feel the weight of his failure to invest in his employees and leaders. His short-sighted belief that it should be good enough that he paid them and offered a basic insurance plan was another fatal mistake.

Secondly, Big Joe didn't connect his presence to the success of the company. "Joe, what you may not see in the ratings is that *showing up and being present nurtures your organization – it's their food source.*" As he stared as the results, Big Joe did not realize how the impact of his absence also drained his employees' morale and motivation.

"Joe, part of your personal change to becoming a successful CEO is understanding the importance of getting to know your employees and leaders – besides your expertise, you are in the people business," I said. "Let's stop here – you have a lot to think about."

> Leaders should influence others in such a way that it builds people up, encourages, and edifies them so they can duplicate this attitude in others.
>
> **Bob Goshen**

Activity: Think about an initiative, improvement, or change you want to implement to fix fatal problems in your business. Using the rating scale of one (1), the lowest to ten (10) the highest, complete the assessment tool to rank your key employees' readiness.

Employee Readiness Assessment

Employee Name	Attribute	Rating
Employee		
	Learning & Development	
	Service & Quality Focus	
	Engagement	
	Job Performance	
	Company Confidence	
	Teamwork	
	Learning & Development	
	Service & Quality Focus	
	Engagement	
	Job Performance	
	Company Confidence	
	Teamwork	
Employee		
	Learning & Development	
	Service & Quality Focus	
	Engagement	
	Job Performance	
	Company Confidence	
	Teamwork	

Employee Name	Attribute	Rating
Employee		
	Learning & Development	
	Service & Quality Focus	
	Engagement	
	Job Performance	
	Company Confidence	
	Teamwork	
Employee		
	Learning & Development	
	Service & Quality Focus	
	Engagement	
	Job Performance	
	Company Confidence	
	Teamwork	

Activity: Based on the results, what are the gaps?_____

_____

_____

_____

_____

_____

_____

_____

Based on your team's readiness assessment, what are key areas to include as part of your 120-day plan to fix your company? _____

_____

_____

_____

_____

_____

BE ABOUT THE BUSINESS

When CEOs and business owners make the fatal mistake of being absent and giving a low-priority to their presence, it quietly erodes the organization's talent and causes employees' low morale and leadership disengagement. Some of the symptoms as a result of CEO absence are:

- **Stress** – Your absence causes frustrations, including uncertainty and burnout, and the workplace is at risk of fostering lawlessness, a hostile workplace, and bullying.
- **Job dissatisfaction** – The cumulative effects of the lack of engagement can ruin employee morale, which can linger for years and invite apathy.
- **Turnover** – When employees become demotivated and feel hopeless, they will seek another workplace where they are appreciated and rewarded.
- **Eats Your Profits** – Absence is expensive. Because your absence destroys job satisfaction, the cost of turnover cuts into profits and productivity.

The following infographic outlines the cause and effect of absent leadership:

As black CEOs and business owners, we do a great job hiring people who look like us. A few of my clients' workforce is predominantly black and consists of workers who, in some cases, find it hard to get a job in mainstream America. Other black workers have a minimum of a bachelor's degree, and over time, their skills are no longer competitive because we do not invest in training, development, and advanced skills. A wise and very profitable CEO once said, " your organization is only as good as the talent and leadership.

I remember reading a Forbes article: *"Top CEOs Sign A Statement Prioritizing People Over Profits: What It Means For Employees."* It mentioned how capitalism has reigned supreme over customers, community, and vendors as lesser priorities. How true is this statement for you?

Although these CEOs are from Fortune 500 companies, I think the shift in their commitment is, at least, a disruptor to think about it. Instead of being driven by the bottom line, pledge to do the following profit-building strategies:

- Deliver value to your customers by meeting or exceeding their expectations.
- Invest in your employees by compensating them fairly, providing benefits, training, and education opportunities. Invite diversity and inclusion of other minority groups, and make it a part of your culture to treat everyone with dignity and respect.
- Deal with fellow minority business owners and suppliers fairly. NEVER ask another small business for free products or services – it devalues their worth. Instead, barter if you can't pay.
- Give back to the communities from which came from, or a black business community. Take time to volunteer and give back – partner with a school to mentor or coach youth to inspire excellence.

BE THE CHANGE

For our next meeting, I created a plan for Big Joe to host his first town hall meeting. I scribbled the plan on a napkin with the following steps:

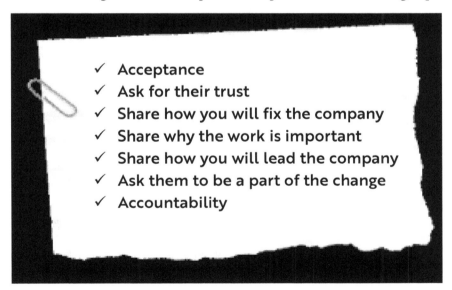

- ✓ Acceptance
- ✓ Ask for their trust
- ✓ Share how you will fix the company
- ✓ Share why the work is important
- ✓ Share how you will lead the company
- ✓ Ask them to be a part of the change
- ✓ Accountability

Big Joe picked up the napkin and stared at it for a while. "I can do this," he said as he smiled and nodded his head in agreement. Joe got up to pace around the room. "Coach, where I come from, I was taught not to own my mistake…just keep moving, don't do it again, and it'll be alright." Pausing to look back at the napkin, he asked, "how in the world am I supposed to stand up in front of my employees to own my mistakes?"

I reminded him, "Joe, you're not the first CEO who had the responsibility to repair the business so it will survive…remember Mr. Seller?" I asked. "No bravado…speak from your heart."

At a Cross Road

When Big Joe met with Ms. Sarah, his executive assistant, to give up an update on what he's been up to and his plan to fix the company, she folded her hands in prayer and whispered, "it's been a long time coming."

"Mr. Joe, how can I help?" she asked.

Ms. Sarah listened to Big Joe and proposed a plan to communicate the town hall meeting and luncheon for all employees. Instead of snacks from the vending machine, Big Joe told Ms. Sarah to have the luncheon catered. "This meeting is the beginning of our future," said Big Joe, "and I want it done right."

To help with the details, Ms. Sarah enlisted the help of the receptionist and administrative assistants to meet her to work through the details. As usual, the receptionist said, "that's not my business." Big Joe overheard the receptionist's comment and walked into the meeting.

The old Big Joe would have humiliated the receptionist in front of the group. Instead, he sat at the table with the group. "Ms. Sarah, I want to hear everyone's ideas on how we can make this a special town hall meeting and luncheon. Who would like to start?"

The receptionist and administrative assistants looked surprised and at a loss for words. With a little bit of coaxing them to speak up, Ms.

Sarah and the group created a plan for the luncheon. They gave Big Joe a budget for the expense. "We all want to chip in and create invitations to the luncheon," said the receptionist. Big Joe applauded the group. "Your enthusiasm is going to help me do my part," he said and thanked them for helping him put the luncheon together. As he left the meeting, several of the employees asked, "Is he for real?"

By the afternoon, the news was buzzing among the employees about Big Joe and how he participated in the meeting to support the plan for the upcoming town hall meeting. Even more shocking was, instead of embarrassing the receptionist for her "not my business" comment, he instead demonstrated teamwork. All of the employees had feared Big Joe and coward dutifully – no one challenged him. If he walked into the breakroom or anywhere, the employees avoided him and returned to their desks.

Some of the employees reacted to the jaw-dropping gossip with excitement, while others said, "Nope, it can't be true." Ms. Sarah smiled and walked with a bounce in her step as she delivered the invitations. One of the last invitations she delivered was to Big Joe's nephew.

Leech was comfortably lounging in his chair with his feet extended on his desk when Ms. Sarah interrupted his solitude with a tap on his leg, and he saw that she'd placed something on his desk. When Leech took off his headphones, he heard laughter and chatter in the breakroom.

Sitting up, Leech picked up the white envelope, peeled back the shiny gold seal to reveal an announcement inside:

Friday, October 19th

Employee Town Hall Meeting

CHANGE AHEAD

CEO
State of the Business Address

Meeting Location: ALS War Room * LUNCH WILL BE SERVED*

Holding the invitation in his hand, he strolled his way to Big Joe's office, found him sitting at a small round table, combing through several reports. "Hey man, what's going on? What's this talk about a town hall meeting?" Leech grimaced. Big Joe pushed back in his chair and asked Leech to sit down. "Well, what do you think," he asked as he motioned for Leech to sit down.

Leech didn't make a move but studied Big Joe's demeanor – something was a little off. He'd never seen his uncle show any interest in anything else but himself, and Leech used that to his advantage. He loved his job because the only requirement was to keep Big Joe informed while he was away. Leech also learned how to feed his Uncle's ego – whatever Big Joe said, did, or questioned, he endorsed it with a "Man, great idea!"

Still standing, Leech asked, "Unk, what's up? Something is off about you. Do you feel alright?" he asked while waving the invitation around in the air. Big Joe sat forward and motioned Leech to sit down. "Leech, well, what do you think?" His nephew sat across from him and rubbed his head in confusion. "Unk, I don't understand…what's is this?"

Big Joe explained that the meeting was a townhall for him to accept ownership of the things he did wrong and to create a clean slate to rebuild the business. "Leech, I am really excited about the future, and now I see a way forward," Leech responded that the company was just fine. "Unk, we don't need to change. That half-a-million is enough to keep you afloat."

Big Joe let out a hearty laugh. "You're kidding me, right?"

"No, I'm not!" Leech was glad to see the Rainmaker and his pinheads leave – good riddance. "We have enough money to keep the company going. Honestly, you can get rid of the dead weight, scale back," Leech yelled! "No town hall meeting is necessary – everything is fine!"

"Are you kidding me?!" Big Joe was having a hard time figuring out if Leech was serious or pulling his leg. "Leech, if I don't do something NOW, there will be no company in six months. I have to take responsibility and make a change." Leech stood up, knocking the chair backward in the process. He stormed out of the room. Perplexed, Big Joe said, "What the hell?" He leaned back from the table, and his thoughts were racing in his head. He went over to his desk and dialed Ms. Sarah's extension. "When you have a moment, please come to my office," he asked.

As Ms. Sarah walked towards Big Joe's office, her heartbeat raced, and thoughts rumbled around in her head. Talking to herself, she wondered if she made a mistake, spent too much money, and stepped out of bounds when she called the meeting with the administrative support team.

"Come in, Ms. Sarah," Big Joe asked and motioned for her to sit in the chair at this desk. "Mr. Joe, did I do something wrong? If I did, I didn't mean any harm, and I can fix it. Just tell what I did, please," she asked softly.

"Ms. Sarah, relax." Softening his tone, Big Joe told her that he was proud of her initiative to organize the town meeting and encouraged her to stop feeling like she was walking on eggshells. "It's my fault you feel that way, and I am so sorry. Let's turn over a new leaf…agree?" he asked. Ms. Sarah smiled and exhaled a big sigh of relief.

"Ms. Sarah, you are a wise person. Tell me your impression of Leech," Big Joe asked. Her mood changed, and frown lines cracked her heavily made-up face. Clearing her throat, she asked, "Mr. Joe, isn't Leech your nephew?" Big Joe nodded agreeably but told Ms. Sarah that his relationship with Leech should not stop her from answering his question.

Ms. Sarah sat tall in the chair and looked directly in Big Joe's eyes. "Mr. Joe, I don't think he means good by you, or anyone. Leech doesn't help his team with the workload. He loafs around most of the day and sits in the lounge area with headphones in his ears. Few employees like Leech, but they tolerate him because he lets everyone know that he is your nephew, and what will happen to them if they piss him off," Ms. Sarah explained. Big Joe excused her.

Her comments reminded him why he hadn't wanted to hire Leech but had felt obligated to his aunt. He knew Leech was trifling, but Joe didn't help matters by making Leech a snitch to keep him informed. Joe stopped back over at Leech's desk. "Leech, come back over to my office."

They took the seats they had earlier vacated. "Yeah, man…what do you want?"

"Leech, we need to find a new way to work together. I did wrong by you by not having any expectations for you to work and help your team. What's even worse is that I created bad relations between you and your coworkers. If I wasn't absent and the leader I needed to be, I think the company wouldn't be in this situation," Big Joe said to his nephew.

Leech replied, "Unk, I don't feel no kinda way with things the way they are. I am just fine."

"Well, Leech, that's not enough." Big Joe told Leech he was going to talk about his plan in the town hall meeting, and added, "I hope you are willing to participate…I need all hands on deck." His nephew stood up and walked away, mumbling to himself.

Activity: Did Big Joe handle Leech's conduct correctly?

_____

_____

_____

_____

_____

_____

What would you do differently? _____

_____

_____

_____

_____

_____

What possibly are consequences of Big Joe's or your own approach to responding to Leech's conduct?

_____

_____

_____

_____

_____

_____

THE POWER OF APOLOGY

Ms. Sarah and the administrative support team looked at their work to organize the town hall meeting. The chairs were arranged in a semi-circle, and the podium where Mr. Joe would stand was centered between both ends of the war room. The windows let in a lot of natural light, and the clouds shielded the sun rays so the audience wouldn't be distracted by the light beams. Ms. Sarah turned on the CD player that played jazz softly in the background. Today was perfect for a new way.

As the employees, supervisor, and the two other leaders assembled in the room, Big Joe and I reviewed his agenda for the meeting. As uncomfortable as he felt to apologize and ask his team to trust him to fix the company, Big Joe was equally excited about the challenge to save the company.

"Joe, this is a huge step for you, the company, and your employees," I said. One of your strengths is your gift-of-gab. Be sincere, but let it connect it to your employees' despair and hopes. For those who are skeptical, win them over one by one." Big Joe inhaled and exhaled to even his breathing.

"One more thing," I added. "For the tough questions, don't get defensive. Acknowledge their concern, say how your plan will address their concerns and ask for them to be a part of the change." Big Joe belted out a hearty laughter. "Coach, if my mom and pop could see me self-deprecating and being humbling to my employees, they would probably call the police and have me arrested.

"Joe, why would you say such a thing?" I asked. He belted out another round of laughter.

"Because whoever this new guy is, they would think he is an imposter!" As much as I tried not to laugh, my buttoned-up persona gave way to his. Our laughter was drowned out by clapping hands. "Joe, that's your cue."

Joe walked tall down the long hallway adorned with the most exquisite black artwork of successful black business owners—beautiful portrayals that captured their strength, determination, courage, and success.

As he stood in the doorway of the war room, Big Joe paused, and the clapping faded to a few hands, which were Ms. Sarah and the administrative support team still cheering for Big Joe as he continued to the podium.

In front of the podium, soberly, he stood and surveyed the faces of his employees. In the back of the room, he saw Leech and his Vice President pacing back and forth, and facing each other to whisper. He returned his attention to the rest of the employees who were eager to hear from him.

"Thank you all for attending our very first town hall meeting. I wish it were to celebrate an outstanding year, and it's not. We will by next year, and we will continue to have more town hall meetings to keep you informed. Today is a way forward." Big Joe looked around the room and saw the faces of his employees brighten up, and some turned to nod that they liked what they heard.

"Before I talk about my plan, I want to say something to each of you," and he paused to gather his thoughts. "I want to sincerely apologize for all the wrong, selfish things I did to bring this company down. My behavior was disrespectful and hurtful. I lost my way, and my ego got in the way, and I was only concerned about what I believed I was entitled to have. I thought I was entitled to the privileges of success because I worked hard to build this company. He's no longer here, but I used my position to take advantage of the Rainmaker – he wanted so much for all of you. I stood in the way. Can you accept my apology and trust me to rebuild the company?" The Vice President walked from the back of the room, clapping his hands to accept Big Joe's apology. One by one, each employee started clapping, and in unison, Big Joe received a standing ovation.

Big Joe motioned everyone to sit down. As he pulled out his notes from his lapel pocket, he scanned the room to find Leech – he was gone. Unbeknownst to him, Ms. Sarah had taken his notes and put them in a PowerPoint. "I thought it would be better for you to show your plan this way," she said. Ms. Sarah handed him the clicker and turned on the widescreen television.

As Big Joe presented his plan, I left the room to find Leech. He was lying down in the employee lounge with his headphones over his ears. I tapped him on his arm. "Leech, why aren't you in the town hall meeting?" I asked him.

He looked angry. He sat up and asked, "Why did you have to come here and change things up? He doesn't need you."

Setting aside that Leech is selfish and takes more than he gives, his reactions to the changes Big Joe is making is one of several behavioral responses. The steps Big Joe took to make changes to save his company are shifting the norm from *content* to *discontent*. I liken this example to how my grandmother would disrupt my cozy sleep snuggled between handmade quilts on a cold Saturday morning. When sweet coaxing to get out of bed didn't work, that woman would yank the covers away for the frigid cold air to disrupt the warmth and content I loved. The warmth of the blankets felt so good that a hot plate of fish and grits – my favorites foods – wouldn't entice me to get up! I am sure you can relate to a time when you felt content and the feelings you experienced when a change made you feel discontent.

In order for change to be successful, it is necessary to break patterns and themes that risk the change or turn-around to save the company. Business owners and CEOs can expect the following uncertainties employees feel during when you move them from a state of content to discontent:

STATUS	Our hardwired social need for esteem and respect, and about our relative importance to others.
CERTAINTY	Our ability to predict what will happen next. When the situation is unfamiliar, trying to make sense of it takes more neural energy.
AUTONOMY	Our sense of control over events and the opportunity to make choices.
RELATEDNESS	The level of comfort and safety we feel with others. We're hardwired to classify people quickly as either friend or foe.
FAIRNESS	A perception of fair exchanges between people.

Dr. David Rock – SCARF Model, NeuroLeadership Institute

Activity: Why do you think Leech resisted what Big Joe wants to do to turn the company around? _____

_____

_____

_____

_____

_____

Now was not the right time to have a conversation with Leech. Just in time, I stepped back into the meeting as Big Joe was taking questions from the audience. What I observed was a CEO who made some tough decisions to get to this day. The employees were excited and the VP stood in the front of the room behind Big Joe. The energy in the room was electric, and everyone was eager to get started.

Closing out the meeting, Big Joe thanked them for their support. "Ms. Sarah will be contacting you next week with more details." While the employees dined, Big Joe and I met to debrief.

"Great meeting Joe. Did you accomplish your goal?"

Joe pulled out his plan and checked this step. Nodding his head, he asked, "what's next?"

Big Joe took a big step to repair his company. It's tough for business owners and CEOs to apologize – it is perceived to weaken the ability to lead and make critical decisions. I differ with that point of view.

The BHFL executive coaching program helps CEOs to understand better how to leverage the power of this behavior. I believe an apology offers an opportunity to take responsibility for wrong-doing, express concerns, and convey the company's values. Secondly, it is an opportunity to sign a psychological contract with employees, customers, and business partners to hold yourself accountable for doing your part to make amends. Thirdly, an apology conveys intention and willingness to change your behavior and the company's culture. If the business owner or CEO can't or doesn't want to do things differently in the future, the case for making an apology is weak, and neither the leadership team nor employees will have a reason to change their behavior or engage.

Activity: Write down an event or something you did that de-serves an apology. _____

_____

_____

_____

Utilize the following table to prepare your apology:

1. What did you do that harmed your organization?
2. How did your conduct affect the employees?
3. What can you do to correct the wrong you did?
4. What actions/behaviors can you demonstrate to show self-accountability?
5. How did your conduct impact your company?
6. How did your conduct impact your company culture?
7. What actions/changes can you take to repair the damage?

Once you complete this exercise, what is your next step?

_____

_____

_____

_____

TRANSFORMATION

The following Monday morning, Big Joe arrived early at the office for our appointment. The receptionist greeted me with a warm smile. "Hello! How are you this morning?" she asked. I told her I couldn't help noticing a warm, welcoming, which is different from what I was used to. She smiled sheepishly. "Yes, your observation is right. I feel great about all the changes Mr. Joe is doing for the company and the employees. I was so afraid that I would be unemployed in a couple of months. I really do like my job and the company." She asked me to take a seat while she let Mr. Joe know I was in the lobby.

Big Joe was dressed in business casual, sleeves rolled up, and on a mission to reach the first milestone. "Coach, come on back…we have a lot to work through today." I made a mental note that he was fully engaged.

Big Joe mapped out his plan on the whiteboard. He put a team together to help him define the company's core values and strengths. "To my surprise, my Vice President stepped up to lead this phase… amazing," Joe said with pride.

After he walked me through his plan to accomplish the tasks, I advised him to be prepared to manage conflict. "What do you mean? Everything is going according to plan," Joe said.

"Yes, so far, so good, but as we put changes in place to improve and repair the company, the process strains conditions that are norms, regardless of whether they are good or bad," I said. I explained to Big Joe that, as a result of his absence and abdicating his authority, the company culture turned toxic and entrenched itself profoundly, and it became another reason for the company's demise. I share with Big Joe what I discovered during my assessment of his culture:

- In-fighting, gossiping, and cliques
- Poor communication and unclear expectations
- Dictatorial management techniques that don't embrace employee feedback
- Excessive absenteeism, disengagement
- Discriminatory policies/wage gaps
- Unhealthy work/life balance
- Unrealistic workloads or deadlines
- Minimum interactions between employees and management

"Joe, what are some things you discovered in your 1:1 interviews? Did any of these things surface?" I asked. After a few minutes, he mentioned he's been aware of these issues but never dealt with them.

To ensure the change initiative is successful, I told Big Joe some strategies we would use to manage and diffuse toxic behaviors.

Here are some strategic remedies to many of the most common workplace problems:

Action	Action/Expectation
Listen to Employees	Along with yourself, expect your managers to have 1:1 coaching sessions or team meetings to listen to their grievances, validate their concerns, and make immediate changes necessary to address their concerns.
Make Workloads and Deadlines Realistic	Invite the employee to provide input in scheduling deadlines – let them take responsibility as much as possible.
Communicate Openly	Employees can't do their jobs well without understanding the context. Having the information to do one's job reduces confusion and frustration, making employees happier and more efficient. Hold weekly meetings, and send frequent memos or a company newsletter. Share the information they need to know.
Share the Spotlight	Hold your managers accountable for finding ways to show appreciation. Tell employees what they're doing well – build a supportive environment by sharing individual and team successes.
Treat All Employees by the Same Rules	Favoritism breeds resentment. Implement HR policies and procedures. Be open to feedback – employees may see problems that you don't. Expect all employees to follow the rules.
Foster Good Relations	Prohibit incivility, disrespect, and dismissive behaviors. Provide resources to help employees expand their emotional intelligence and ways to resolve conflict and find ways to compromise.

Big Joe wrote down notes to add to his plan. As a note to himself, he wrote: "*What I did not include as part of my plan is training my managers on the changes I expect them to implement.*" He called Ms. Sarah to schedule a meeting for the supervisors and VP next week.

Activity: Today you are Big Joe's coach. How would you advise him to use the list of remedies to help Leech accept the changes Big Joe is implementing to fix the company?

_____

_____

_____

_____

_____

How would you advise Big Joe if Leech is not willing to at least try to participate in the change initiatives?

_____

_____

_____

_____

_____

_____

Before our session ended, Big Joe mentioned he had more good news. In order to bring in new business, he was going to cut his salary by 50% to hire a new business developer and CFO. He outlined an aggressive plan to add three new contracts by year end. Big Joe realized he made a fatal mistake when he stopped contacting his customers and meeting new prospective customers – he had left it up to the Rainmaker.

Mentally, Big Joe was exhausted by the end of the day, but it all felt gratifying. He was thankful that his employees were on board and willing to give him a chance to fix the problems he caused. The one issue weighing on him was Leech.

Breakthrough

The next morning, Big Joe arrived to work early again, and the employees began to take note that he'd been coming in early and consistently. Each morning he arrived, he was pleasant and greeted each employee as they arrived. He wanted them to see he was on time, and he expected them to be on time. At least once a week, the employees smelled fresh coffee aroma coming from the employee lounge. Big Joe sat in the lounge, drinking his coffee, and chatting with the employees. "Tell me something," he asked Ms. Sarah. "What do you think about a communication board in here to keep the employees informed? I would need your help to make updates and shout outs." Ms. Sarah was glad to help.

Big Joe left the lounge and looked across the way to see if Leech was at his desk. The rest of his teammates were busy working but no sign of his nephew. Big Joe walked over and left a note on his monitor

When Leech finally arrived at work, it was nearly noon. The receptionist called him to her desk. "Your Uncle wants you to come to his office," she said as she raised her eyebrows to express concern. The receptionist noticed that since Mr. Joe had been working to save the company, Leech had been feeling some kind of way.

Leech heard what she said, but he couldn't care less why his Uncle wanted to see him. As long as his check was deposited in his bank on time, he wanted no part of "the change." He strolled over to his desk and saw a note posted to his monitor. Leech pulled it off and threw it in the trash. "Oh, smack," laughed Rafael, who worked on the tech support team with Leech. "Man, what's up with you? What's wrong, your Unk is putting pressure on you to do some work?" Rafael and the other techies laughed at Leech. They didn't like him because he was trifling and wouldn't do anything to help the team when the call volume got high.

Leech walked away and went to the employee lounge to stretch out on one of the sofas. He put his headphones and pressed play to hear *Cam'ron - I Hate My Job.* Leech turned up the volume to drown out his fear of the changes on the horizon, and he didn't want to punch a clock and do stuff that would measure his performance, or how he got along with the dicks in his department. He earned his pay keeping his uncle informed – Leech looked forward to this shit being over and was ready for his uncle to go back to being himself again. Leech convinced himself all "this stuff" was just an act to rally the knuckleheads to believe him. Once the company was stable again, his uncle would leave for another trek, and he would be back in control and needed by Big Joe. But for now, he was pissed at Big Joe.

Startled by a sudden tap on his shoulder, Leech sat up on his elbows and looked around to see who disturbed his zone. "Oh, it's you."

Big Joe sat on the soft polka dot, mushroom-style stool. "Leech, I don't know what's going on with you but we need to get to the bottom of it. You checked out on me, and I don't have the faintest idea why," Big Leech said, scratching the stubble itching his chin.

Leech sat up. "Man, I was your boy. I kept you informed and kept everyone in check when you were out doing whatever you did. Me – I was your eyes and ears. That was my job."

Big Joe listened to his nephew. His nephew was afraid of how the changes will affect his job. "Leech, everyone has to change if we're going to save the company. Did you know I cut my salary in half to hire people to help me find new customers? Did you notice I don't dress flashy anymore – those days are gone. I have a responsibility to keep this company going, so I have to make sacrifices and change."

Leech jumped up from the couch. "If you change, then I don't have a job," he growled. "I don't have a job!"

Big Joe explained he always had a job, but he never expected him to do it. "Leech, I was so wrapped up into what I was doing, and didn't care much about what was happening as long as I could do what I enjoyed – I felt entitled and everything else was damned. Working with BHFL Group is not only fixing the business issues – it's helping me to look at my behaviors and beliefs. I couldn't see how my selfishness impacted not only the business but also the lives of my employees. I have to take responsibility to fix the damage I caused. I need your help, but if you can't support what I need to do to save the company, leave."

Activity: Why do you think Leech is resisting change?

_____

_____

_____

_____

_____

_____

_____

_____

Bravery is not the absence of fear but the
forging ahead despite being afraid.

Robert Liparulo

As a change practitioner, I've seen so many of my clients struggle with change. Business owners and CEOs know they have to change, but these are the three things that keep them stuck. They are:

- Afraid of the unknown
- Used to behaviors and systems that have been honed over time and have received positive rewards
- Convinced that "how it used to be" will save them

There are many more, but these are three reasons why it is so tricky for CEOs, business owners, and employees to realize that their growth is limited and often self-imposed in their minds because of fear and unwillingness to step out of their comfort zone. In other words, the past limits what they "see" in the present. Here are three more reasons why change is difficult:

- **Habits are powerful and efficient.** The older we get, the harder it is to rewire our mind map – we get stuck in a rut. Our brain resists new ways of doing things, and we revert to pass behaviors. A simple exercise in learning how to be adaptable is trying new foods that aren't in your repertoire. Because we live in an instantaneous world, agility is necessary to be relevant.
- **Our brain is not wired for change!** It is a plus when you need to recall information stored in our brain, but not so good when there is a need to learn something new or do something different.
- **We have to act – see and feel – on new ways of doing things if the change is going to stick.** Adopting new behaviors and sustaining them over time are the results of learning. The more you learn, the more your brain changes, building new mind maps for making decisions, innovations, and creations. Fixing

fatal mistakes requires thinking and doing things differently and challenging old ways of thinking and being.

Rewards of Change

One of my favorite songs by Sam Cooke, *A Change is Gonna Come*, is my anthem for letting go of learned behavior growing up poor. Despite my grandparents doing the best they could, every day was a challenge to make enough money to keep food on the table, and I had to leave the neighborhood to go to college. Leaving home was the first great change I faced with fear. But I did it. We all can change behaviors and beliefs that limit our growth.

Big Joe learned to use his hustle to get what he wanted – it landed him his first major contract. However, the more successful he became, the more he disconnected with mindfulness.

Six Months Later

Through hard work and determination, Big Joe had taken his company from hanging on by a thread to winning a new contract. With a successful close out of the change initiative and with a new $4.5 million contract, Big Joe celebrated and gave each employee a bonus for trusting him to fix the fatal mistakes and putting policies and procedures in place to make sure every employee is treated fairly.

He recognized Ms. Sarah for her loyalty, despite working as a temp employee for so many years. In addition to her bonus, he promoted Ms. Sarah to the Operations Manager to oversee daily operations. In turn, she created an ALS Ambassador Team, which included the receptionist and the administrative assistants. Her team was responsible for maintaining the leaderboard that communicated how each team was performing and accomplishing goals and posting Mr. Joe's shout-outs and accolades to recognize employees. Ms. Sarah also partnered with the managers to schedule training events to ensure all employees had the skills and capabilities to meet the demands of their job.

Today is the final session to close out our contract. When I walked into ALS, it felt so different from the first time I came. The receptionist was busy taking calls, and she did it with a smile instead of a snarl. Behind the glass partition of her desk, I could see energetic people walking, meeting, and answering calls. The Vice President of Marketing rebranded the company using the core values all employees helped to define, and ALS designed a new logo to help announce the company's transformation.

"Joe, how are you? I can't believe the transformation I see with my very own eyes. Your employees looked oppressed during my first meeting, and now they are confident, proud, and struttin' their stuff – look at them, Joe," I said, hardly believing my eyes. "Give yourself a pat on the back – you did it!"

He humbly smiled and gave all the praise to his leadership team and employees. The old Big Joe would have lapped up the compliment and then asked for more.

"Hey, do you have time to walk with me," he asked. I would like for you to see what the employees gave to me as a gift," and we continued to talk about all that he and his team accomplished.

I noticed all the high tech computers and gadgets were well used, and some desktops were "decorated" with coffee stains, scribbled on note pads, and markers and pins tossed about at random. The tech team wore portable headsets that allowed them to decrease the calls in the queue – they could answer inbound calls anywhere in the loft.

I followed Big Joe to a glass wall inscribed

CHANGE
is the food of champions!

As he looked proudly at the inscription, Joe rocked back on his heels and folded his arms across his chest. "My employees collected money to have an artist create this as a gift to me and to say thank you for saving the company and their jobs. It's incredible. My daily ritual is to start each day with a stand-up meeting in front of this wall and state our mission and vision, and where we want to be as a company in the next two years. Amazingly, they are all on board!" Big Joe was elated and proud of his team.

He took me to the next stop of our tour, and I noticed the desk where Leech seat was vacant. "Joe, with all of the positive energy and work you are doing, is Leech still coming in late?" I asked.

As we walked into the war room, Big Joe paused with silence. He felt responsible that he was not able to get Leech to see how the change would benefit him. "Unfortunately, Leech decided to quit – he just stopped coming to work, and I didn't try to bring him back. Sometimes, it's best to let bygones be bygones."

Big Joe pivoted to show me several matrices of bid opportunities in the pipeline. He laughed, "I remembered when I wouldn't come in this room! It was another fatal mistake not to take any interest in the work that kept the lights on!" I looked at the matrices he developed and now monitors with the CFO and business development team.

"How are you doing with your business relationships with the contracting officers – you lost contact with them when you relied on the Rainmaker to be your proxy," I said with caution, knowing that mentioning that name still caused him angst.

Big Joe walked over to the table to sit. "One more thing I need to share with you. Out of all the good I accomplished with my team, something still felt hollow. While I sat in church with my mom and pop, I realized I needed to make amends for all the horrible things I did to him." Big Joe explained that he had decided to call the Rainmaker to schedule a private meeting.

"Did he accept?" I asked,

Big Joe said the Rainmaker hadn't responded to his invitation, but he is hopeful.

We wrapped up the tour and walked back to his office to review my closeout action items and schedule a one-year follow-up date.

LESSONS LEARNED

After I returned to my office, I thought about Joe's conversation and his feelings of despair for not having an opportunity to make amends with the Rainmaker – perhaps I could help.

The following day, I called the Rainmaker, and he invited me to meet him at his office. As I walked up Peachtree Street, I thought it was uncanny that his office was about five blocks from Big Joe.

When I arrived, I was pleasantly greeted by the Rainmaker's receptionist, and she escorted to his office. From behind a mahogany desk, a conservatively dressed man with manicured hands stood to greet me. The Rainmaker stood up to shake my hand and asked the receptionist to bring both of us a coffee. "If you don't mind, now and then, I enjoy a cup of coffee in the afternoon to *change* things up," he said with a smile.

I explained to the Rainmaker why I requested the meeting, and asked for his confidence not to share with Big Joe that I met with him.

"I don't talk to him anymore, so you don't need to worry about that," said the Rainmaker. His tone changed from relaxed to irritated. "Have you heard any gossip about Big Joe and all the changes he's personally made, as well as those he made to turn the business around?" I asked.

"No, I haven't. Anytime someone mentions Big Joe's name in my network, I leave. My time at ALS was mostly a painful experience and one that I want to forget.

"I can respect that, and I see you don't have closure as well – that's why I am here," I said.

I explained to the Rainmaker what happened after he left and started his company. "You may not believe this, but Joe doesn't hold any malice towards you and accepts the responsibility that he drove you away. He takes responsibility for how badly he treated you and everyone else at that time. But, I also think it's important for you to know is that he is not the same CEO you knew then."

The Rainmaker sat in awe and was having a hard time moving past, "he takes responsibility." After all, Big Joe had never taken responsibility for anything unless it entitled him more to do what he wanted. "I understand your caution, but people can change, and Joe has changed considerably," I said.

The Rainmaker still didn't say a word. "I will leave you now, but you both need closure – please accept his invitation to meet. You both have some healing to do." I left my business card on the table and extended my hand to bid him goodbye.

When I returned to my office, my desk phone message light was flashing. I pushed the red light, and the virtual assistant said, "you have one unopened message – push one to listen."

"Hello, this is the Rainmaker. I thought about what you said, and I agree. I still have flashbacks of horrible times at ALS – perhaps this meeting will put these bad feelings to rest. I will call Big Joe." *End of message...there are no more unopened messages*. I clicked the button to end the call.

Activity: How would you handle a business relationship that took advantage of you? _____

_____

_____

_____

How would you handle a business relationship where you took advantage of an employee or one of your leaders?

_____

_____

_____

_____

How would you make amends for your actions?

_____

_____

_____

Why is it important to make amends or let the tyrant make amends with you? _____

_____

_____

_____

REDEMPTION

Springtime in Atlanta is a beautiful sight. All the Dogwood trees are in full bloom, and people are buzzing up and down Peachtree Street. While visiting a new client a few blocks north of Peachtree, I ran into the Rainmaker having lunch where I was invited to meet my new client.

He waved at me and motioned me to come over. As I zig-zagged my way between tables and people standing in the middle of the room, it took me a minute or so to get to the booth where the Rainmaker sat enjoying a late lunch with his guest.

Extending my hand, I asked, "How are you?" Before he could answer, I was distracted by a familiar person seated to his left – it was Big Joe sitting in the booth with the Rainmaker. I was speechless for a minute and at a loss for words.

Laughing, the Rainmaker pulled me to sit next to him. He slid over to make room for me.

"Hello, Coach. It's a pleasant surprise to see you," said Big Joe in a playful way.

The Rainmaker motioned to call the server over. "Please bring another glass of water."

He squeezed my arm lightly, I looked across the table at Big Joe and back to my right at the Rainmaker. He cleared his throat. "Come, come now. If you don't say something, I'll think you had a mild stroke," he said jokingly.

"What happened?" I asked.

Big Joe chimed in and told me everything. One day, the Rainmaker returned his call and agreed to meet. He was afraid to face the man he tormented and disrespected for so many years, but Big Joe knew he needed to make amends for all the pain the Rainmaker endured because of him.

Over several private meetings, Big Joe said they talked. "It was tough facing his anger," Joe said, "and to hear how he suffered from physical stress that I caused – his family suffered with him. However painful the experience was for both of us, we agreed to keep talking.

"After the eight or so meetings, we both began to see a turning point and decided to bury our old relationship and, with the Rainmaker's permission, create a new relationship. We both found out that neither of us was the same man from our past – we both changed but for different reasons." Big Joe said they also realized they wanted to help other entrepreneurs, CEOs or business owners who made the same fatal mistakes as Big Joe, and they wanted to be an example for change for those who have lost their way. Big Joe and the Rainmaker host a monthly meeting after hours to share their story and mentor other black business owners and CEOs – they also teach the new start-ups what fatal mistakes to avoid.

The Rainmaker interrupted. "You know, I've heard so many sermons about forgiveness but never experienced a circumstance that challenged me to put it into practice. This life-changing experience with Big Joe taught me how to reconcile and heal, and my bitterness towards him infected my family and my business. Big Joe and I can do more good together than apart." Extending his hands towards the smiling man facing him, the Rainmaker said, "I admire this man – the new Big Joe. I can only imagine the sorrow he felt when he decided he needed to change."

Both men reached across the table to shake hands and affirmed their friendship. I admired the two of them and the work they had both put in together to create a new relationship.

> "Forgiveness says you are given another
> chance to make a new beginning."
>
> **Desmond Tutu**

I have a saying that change manifests itself in many ways, and creeps into the crevices where there the light can not shine. When I start a change management project, they all start with a plan and outcome. But more often than not, the path to change is not a straight path. I begin with assessing the past, comparing it to the present, and helping my client to determine the ideal future state and a way forward from the current business state – this is easier said than done. The path to success oftentimes uncover layers of stuff hidden behind low morale, dissatisfaction, disengagement, hopelessness, and employees feeling devalued.

When I coach and consult with my clients, sometimes our past hinders our ability to embrace change. Instead of fixing fatal mistakes, they become a part of the present and keep showing up like a chronic disease.

In a time when we see powerful examples void of integrity, character, and respect, it's easy to become blinded and caught up in self-indulgence and entitlement. But I implore black business owners and CEOs to take a look at their fatal mistakes and how they impact the business, their employees, and themselves.

When you fix your fatal mistakes, nothing can stop your growth, success, or block your way to the summit.

Activity: What are the fatal mistakes that keep you awake at night? _____

_____

_____

_____

_____

_____

What can you do to change and repair them? _____

_____

_____

_____

_____

_____

FINAL WORDS

Mastering the art to change and being a catalyst for it is a game changer. I hope Big Joe's story and lessons he learned are a beacon to find your way forward. Mistakes can be fatal, but they don't have to be permanent.

Whether your business is in the toilet or not, the roadmap and activities are a great starting point to fix your fatal mistakes.

Whether you are making millions, lost millions, or grinding to make your first million, the agility to change is imperative to remain relevant in today's complex, socially interactive business market. Equally important, CEOs and business owners must invest in building their leadership capabilities and balancing control with humility, confidence, and having a sincere interest in their employees, and becoming a catalyst for change in action. Your stages of personal development as a CEO or business owner are core to leadership effectiveness, emotional intelligence, and remaining relevant over time.

Secondly, implementing change to turn around a failing business or to sustain growth starts with you – when you fix your problems, you will fix your company. You are a reflection of your company, and change is parallel between you and your company.

Big Joe embodied toxic behaviors driven by an unchecked ego that was fed by an unhealthy diet of confidence and control – he lost sight of his aspiration to be a business owner to give people jobs, help his community, and make his father proud. This noble idea was replaced with a belief of entitlement and privilege afforded by success.

Where Do You Start?

If you believe that you are the solution to fix your problems, you can save your company, achieve greater profitability, and inspire your leaders to be great team builders.

> In the black of night, silence finds your conscious
> sullen with disappointment and a fear to change
> You regret that you didn't see a need to change
> Disrobe your ego – let go of content
> Evolve, recreate, discover, and reinvent
> Welcome your greater you!
>
> **Renzie Richardson**

Lightning Source UK Ltd.
Milton Keynes UK
UKHW011247130520
363213UK00002B/475

9 781734 818604